THE FAIRWAY GOURMET

chef Jacky Pluton

THE FAIRWAY GOURMET

chef Jacky Pluton

A CELEBRATION OF GOLF DESTINATIONS & CULINARY DELIGHTS

with Lisa Kahn

Published by
The Fairway Gourmet LLC/Jacky Pluton
1235 A North Clybourn #351
Chicago, Illinois 60610
312-266-1440

Food Photography and Photos of the Chef © Etienne Heimermann
Other Photography: page 12 © Kemper Lake Golf Club;
page 15 © The Hong Kong and Shanghai Hotels, Limited; page 19 © Jacky Pluton;
pages 28 and 37 © Pebble Beach Company; page 46 © Ojai Country Club;
pages 59 and 65 © Wyndham International; pages 74 and 79 © The American Club;
pages 109 and 113 © The Ritz-Carlton Hotel Company, LLC;
pages 124 and 128-129 © Kiawah Island Golf Resort;
pages 140 and 146 © The Lodge at Sea Island; page 158 © The Oak Knoll Inn

Watercolor Paintings © Christian Fanelli

This cookbook is a collection of favorite recipes,
which are not necessarily original recipes.

ISBN: 0-9769714-0-2
Library of Congress Control Number: 2005907315

Edited, designed, and manufactured by
Favorite Recipes® Press
an imprint of

P.O. Box 305142
Nashville, Tennessee 37230
800-358-0560

Book Design: Dave Malone
Art Director: Steve Newman
Project Editor: Jane Hinshaw
Project Manager: Ashley Bienvenu

Manufactured in the United States of America
First Printing: 2005
10,000 copies

DEDICATION

To my wife, Berny, and our children, Clara and Enzo

In loving memory of my mother

PREFACE

I consider myself a lucky man each and every day that I step into my kitchen at my restaurant, Pluton, in Chicago to live out my American dream. Having grown up in France but now living in the United States for nearly twenty years, I think the place that I learned to love this country the most—its vast and gorgeous terrain, delicious and diverse ingredients, and entertaining personalities—was the golf course.

You might think that the golf course is a funny place to find a French chef roaming the United States but au contraire—when I teed up for the first time eighteen years ago in Valley Forge, Pennsylvania, I was hooked forever. That day in Valley Forge, I had never swung a club before, I played with a set of $75 golf clubs that my roommate gave me for my birthday, and I managed to shoot a 210 in six hours flat. My golf game has since seen better days—thankfully—but as I continued to learn the game over the next 18 years, I inevitably found myself in more woods, bushes, and lakes than I care to admit. Now proudly boasting a 22 handicap (the pinnacle of my golf game was a 17 handicap when I lived in Boca Raton, Florida), my golf adventures have led me to the most beautiful places in America, where I have literally stumbled across delicious herbs, fruits, and regional ingredients growing on or around golf courses. And that is how the concept behind *The Fairway Gourmet* was born—a celebration of America's finest golf courses, average golfers, regional ingredients, diverse cultures, and colorful personalities.

Who better to be your tour guide than me—a chef who found a way to marry his two great loves in life— golf and cooking? So join me as I travel the country swinging clubs, savoring newfound flavors, and making lifelong memories. Life is about what we French describe as joie de vivre, the joy of living, and that is what this book celebrates.

Table of Contents

FG

chef
Jacky Pluton

JACKY PLUTON GOURMET CHEF

Jacky Pluton is a world-class chef with a zest for passionate living—and a dream to someday score in the 80s. Born on Table 17 of his father's restaurant in Serrieres, France, Jacky has carried the family tradition of fine cooking to award-winning heights, graduating first in his class from Ecole Hoteliere de la Chaise Dieu. He worked in Michelin-star-rated restaurants in France, Monaco, and Switzerland before coming to the United States in 1986, where he has been Executive Chef at several of this country's top restaurants.

Jacky earned a succession of Five-Star Mobil ratings and Four-Star ratings from a Chicago-area publication. In 1996, he opened the first of several restaurants in the Chicago area and today is the Chef/Owner of Pluton in Chicago.

Jacky, married to Berny for sixteen years and the father of two, lives in Highland Park. His plucky personality and passion for food, wine, culture, travel, motorcycles, and, of course, golf, give *The Fairway Gourmet* a generous blend of lifestyle, wit, exuberance, and fun.

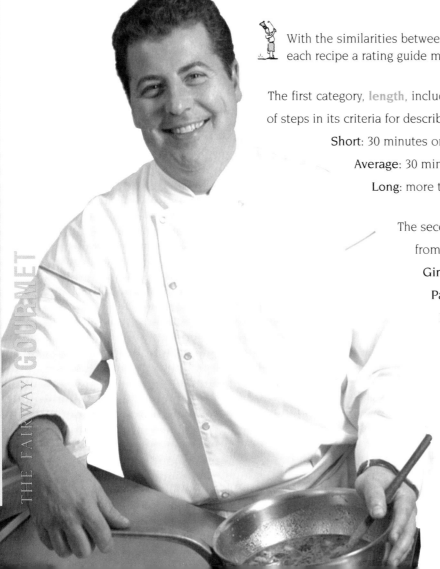

With the similarities between golf and cooking in mind, Jacky has given each recipe a rating guide much as golf courses rate each hole.

The first category, length, includes both preparation time and the number of steps in its criteria for describing each recipe:

Short: 30 minutes or less

Average: 30 minutes to 1 hour

Long: more than 1 hour

The second category ranks the degree of difficulty from the easiest to the most difficult:

Gimme: very easy

Par 3: easy

Par 4: some degree of challenge

Par 5: very challenging

The final category, cost, takes into account the ingredients and any necessary special tool or piece of equipment. The categories are:

Low, Average, or High Greens Fees

Compliments From The Chef

Writing a book is a team effort, and it turns out to be just like opening a restaurant; it takes passion and hard work by many people. I'm very proud of the result.

First, I need to thank Jim Mack, my former partner in The Fairway Gourmet Show, without whose help and knowledge of the industry, *The Fairway Gourmet* would be a project, not a reality. I raise my glass to you.

This book would certainly not exist without the loyalty, support, and vision of the hardest working man in America, Bill Reisthein. Thank you for your patience and all your support for the past four years. Thank you for your expertise in making this project a success.

My television crew was indispensable, putting in long hours as we traveled around the country. Thank you to Lance Catena, Ken Nislsson, Gene Cosentino, Mark Niedlson, Terry Schilling, Doug Mara, Joel, and all the crew at X-Ray Productions.

Many thanks to the staff of Jacky's Bistro and Pluton, and many thanks to Anthony Keravec and Darin Bieck for your help in the kitchen when we took your mise en place.

Thank you, Lisa Kahn, for your help with the words.

Glenn, thanks for your patience. You are a gentleman.

Many thanks to Steve and Nancy Crown.

Merci, Etienne Heimermann, pour votre patience pendant les moments difficiles, merci milles fois.

Aussi merci Christian pour ton coup de pinceau que j'adore de puis mon enfance tu merites toutes les accolades pour ta peinture, bisous et bonne santé.

Last but not least, a big thanks to my family for their love and wholehearted support of this latest project.

From Lisa Kahn CO-AUTHOR

The completion of this adventure in touring, golfing, cooking, and writing would not have been possible without the gracious assistance of the countless people we worked with along our way to every travel destination. My sincere thanks go out to those who arranged for our explorations on and off the golf course and to those who patiently answered every question we shot out, no matter how odd it may have seemed at the time! A project of this magnitude is never a singular achievement, and the thoughtful input and generous support of many people have seasoned the pages of this book. I would like to acknowledge Anthony Keravec, Chef de Cuisine at Pluton, and Luanne Caringal from the Bistro and Pluton, for their conscientious assistance with the recipes, and Darin Bieck from Jacky's Bistro for his contributions early on in this endeavor. I am most grateful to my friend Kathe Telingator for not only lending me her eyes to read through preliminary drafts, but also for her professional expertise, her ear, and shoulders of support.

I am truly indebted to many dear friends whose interest in this project went far beyond the occasional inquiry. Many acted as guinea pigs, willingly and good-naturedly tasting concoctions of would-be recipes. My sincere and heartfelt thanks go out to Jaime and Mee Kim-Chavez, Wolfgang and Regina Kuehne-Erfeld, Christos and Stassa Komissopoulos, and Dan Mitchell, all of whose genuine enthusiasm and approach to life has kept me on course. I can't think of a more congenial place to write than Savories on Wells, a personal favorite local destination. My thanks to Violeta Woodward and the whole Monday morning gang who always saved me a spot next to the outlet and filled the place with true joie de vivre.

Lastly, I want to individually thank my family for their interest in this project and support for me to accomplish the tasks at hand, be they far away or in our very own kitchen! Thanks to my mom, Stevie Sorensen (a wonderful cook, a faithful friend, and a computer guru); my dad, Herb Sherman; my other parental units, Sandy and Corky Kahn and Chuck Sorensen; and sibs Greg and Dana Sherman, Peter and Sonia Sorensen, Kristen Sorensen, Julie Landau, and Ken Young. To my girls, Kylie and Quincy, I will be eternally grateful for your help in the kitchen, for your ability to roll with whatever requirements this project threw our way, and for your love. And to my husband, Glenn, I thank you for unequivocally believing in this endeavor and in me.

ABOUT LISA KAHN

A Scottsdale, Arizona, native, Lisa received a Bachelor of Arts from Lake Forest College and a Master of Arts in the History of Architecture and Art from the University of Illinois at Chicago. She worked in the fine arts as an art appraiser and museum assistant curator, and taught art history at the college level before turning her interests to the culinary arts and writing. She holds a Diploma of French Cuisine from the Centre Formation Alternee de la Ville de Cannes, France. A member of the Chicago Culinary Historians, Lisa makes her home in Chicago, with her husband and two daughters.

Introduction

I remember the moment that the idea for this book was born. I was on the 17th fairway at the Ojai Country Club's course in Ojai, California. The scent of lavender perfumed the summer breeze. The late afternoon sun illuminated the ridges of the Topa Topa Mountains, which cradled the course. Still basking in the exquisite day of friendship and sport, my party glided to the 18th tee, and my passion for golf began to connect with my instincts as a chef. Would tonight's dinner start with a '98 Santa Barbara County Gainey Chardonnay or a '99 Anderson Valley Goldeneye Pinot Noir? Would the crown jewel of this regal day be spotted prawns and carrots en papillote or short ribs with seven spices wine sauce?

I wanted to hold on to this day and savor every second. A book seemed to be the perfect means with which to record these triumphal days so that I could recall them and replay them—in memory and in reality. A book would also allow me to share these special times with home cooks and aesthetes alike, who have the same quest for living life with gusto.

My own adventure with food began when my mother gave birth to me on Table 17 at my father's restaurant in France. I was raised by an active extended family. My grandparents kept apple and cherry orchards and took me blueberry hunting. We frequently foraged for chanterelles and cèpes. My maternal grandparents made wine, raised game, and canned a variety of products each year. The smell of pickles, like the ones they used to make, still conjures to mind images of boisterous activity and true conviviality. My upbringing has truly shaped my desire to bring joy and pleasure to shared occasions. My book concept is essentially an extension of what I have always believed as a restaurateur.

The restaurant business is not simply about food and wine; it is about one's experiences and pleasures, be it a celebration following the victories of the week or a palliative offering after a daily struggle or defeat. The restaurateurs that I have worked beside understand the underlying magical combinations that fulfill the clientele's desire for joie de vivre—the joy of living. From La Tasse in Lyon and Le Clovis in Paris to Trouvaille in New York and Jacky's Bistro, my casual café north of Chicago, my aim has always been to bring about this heightened experience for my diners. The purpose of this book is to bring this richness of experience, especially in a culinary sense, to everything that surrounds the leisure activity that so many people love—the game of golf.

This book not only celebrates joie de vivre, it pursues it with passion. If your love of travel, wine, fine dining, beauty, and—one of the ultimate worldly pleasures—golf is akin to mine, this is an invitation to enjoy the journey together.

MY HOMETOWN
CHICAGO
Illinois

Sunrise on the 12th hole
on Kemper Lake Golf Club
in Long Grove, Illinois.

When It Comes To Chicago,

the likelihood of finding delicious

food, great golf, and true hospitality is very high.

Regardless of whether you are willing and able to spend a lot or are looking to spend very little, you can bet that you will find consistency in friendly service and quality products here. From haute cuisine and high-caliber 18-hole courses to ethnic street foods, unique pars 3s, miniature courses, and driving ranges, Chicago offers some of the best from both of these worlds. Come to Chicago and explore some of my hometown favorites!

If I had to select from among the many options for hotels in my city, I can't think of a better choice to reflect the true spirit of Chicago than The Peninsula. Located off Michigan Avenue in the very heart of Chicago, which locals call "The Magnificent Mile," The Pen is quintessentially luxurious; its spacious art deco surroundings echo Chicago's architectural legacy and create the perfect setting for the gracious service that makes one's stay here so memorable. The Peninsula prides itself on its friendly Midwestern hospitality and a willingness to always go the extra mile for its guests. Not only has The Peninsula earned my high praise; it has won professional accolades since it opened its doors three years ago, raising Chicago to the gold standard for a travel destination. In addition to earning a AAA 5-Diamond Award and the Mobil 5-Star Award for 2004, The Peninsula was rated by *Travel & Leisure* as Number One in the United States and Canada in their prestigious "World's Best Awards 2004" and "World's Best Service 2004."

A Hong Kong–based company with an eye on the global market, The Peninsula also celebrates Chicago's own multicultural population, and its restaurants reflect this diversity. My favorites are Pierrot Gourmet, an authentic French café complete with sidewalk tables for the ultimate in urban people-watching while enjoying a coffee, and Shanghai Terrace, a hip and upscale dining space that features Pan-Asian specialties.

At Shanghai Terrace, diners are immediately welcomed into the special atmosphere by a staff who shares a deep respect for the tradition of dining at table. Diners are encouraged to take their time to sit and experience a fine meal, and formal elements are vital to achieving this full experience. The

prepares. From the tiniest kitchen I think I have ever seen, Chef Chen and his crew crank out an amazing number of stellar dishes! Some of my favorite dim sum are the dumplings—both pork and lobster—the crystal shrimp pot stickers, turnip cakes whose sweetness is well balanced by a crisp but nongreasy exterior, the scallop shu mai, the peeky toe crab won tons, and the bean curd sheets with chicken and mushroom ragout.

With the warmer months comes a slightly different feel to the dining experience at Shanghai Terrace, where they offer a seasonally inspired menu. If weather permits, sit outside to nibble on their delicacies; it is the only outdoor dim sum I know! The terrace is also a cool place to sit and relax with a

If you like chocolate, The Pen is the place to be.

reserved atmosphere and unobtrusive but highly attentive service is anything but stuffy; rather, a meal at Shanghai Terrace is reflective of a warm and gracious staff whose art of fine service is equal to the exquisitely prepared food. How many times have you dined on delicious food only to have the experience compromised by inept service? Here, the dining experience is seamless.

Choose from an extensive list of appetizers and main dishes off the à la carte menu at Shanghai Terrace, or if it is lunchtime, consider a delicious bento tray special or dim sum. I like to experience the broad spectrum of menu items when I dine out, and choosing a chef's tasting menu is a great way to do just that. Like tapas in Spanish cuisines, the gorgeously presented, precious dim sum bites are the best way to sample the wide array of Asian fare that Chef Richard Chen deftly

cocktail outdoors. Spectacular views of Chicago from this fourth floor spot include the Water Tower, one of the few buildings to survive Chicago's big fire in 1871, and the John Hancock Building, a modern skyscraper that reminds me of a small Sears Tower. It's like a primer in Chicago architecture right under your nose!

The desserts at Shanghai Terrace deserve special mention as well. The lemon grass panna cotta comes surrounded by a serene circle of pistachio foam and seasonal fresh fruit. It's light and refreshing. On the other end of the spectrum is the chocolate ravioli paired with a dollop of vanilla sorbet. I love how the sorbet melts into a pool of fresh strawberry soup. It's so delicious that I soaked up every last drop of it with a delicate lemon madeleine! Equally decadent is the fried white chocolate cheesecake, whose molten interior literally bursts out of its crispy wrapper.

If you like chocolate, The Pen is the place to be on Friday and Saturday nights between 8:00 P.M. and 11:30 P.M. for its chocolate bar. You can indulge yourself at their signature chocolate buffet featuring 26 white, milk, and dark chocolate creations ranging from tiny pastries to sinful chocolate creams, all

Though I do love to travel and have been extremely lucky to play many of the top golf courses in the United States, I'm equally content exploring the vast golf resources that exist in my own town. Some of the best golf in the country is located within a 50-mile radius of Chicago. A favorite course of mine

The gallery of The Peninsula hotel features the art deco era of Chicago's architectural history, while the hotel's restaurants celebrate the city's cultural diversity.

THE PENINSULA

made in-house. Be sure to make a reservation, as it can get busy. If the desserts alone don't blow you away, you will be awed by the 20-foot-high floor-to-ceiling windows that overlook North Michigan Avenue. The grand lobby also features live jazz and a dance floor to work off that chocolate-induced energy, so enjoy the evening, but save something for the next day when phenomenal golf awaits.

is Kemper Lakes Golf Club. Located in Long Grove, Illinois, it's an easy hour's drive northwest from downtown Chicago.

If you're staying at The Peninsula, before departing for Kemper, consider having some light fare packed to go at Pierrot Gourmet. Or make a quick detour downtown to Bari Foods on Grand Avenue, where brothers Frank and Ralph Pedota make a killer sub

Though I do love to travel and have been extremely lucky to play many of the top golf courses in the United States...

sandwich from bread made at D'Amaot's Bakery next door. Try adding their mild or hot giardiniera for the full-flavor experience. Wrapped in white butcher paper, this sandwich will happily keep for the return ride if you have the willpower to wait to sink your teeth into it! The guys always cut the sandwiches in two, so I usually eat half before playing and save the other half for the ride home.

The vestige of a once-thriving Italian neighborhood on Grand Avenue is full of delicious and authentic Italian specialties. The guys at this family-run grocery store make their own sausage, butcher their own meats to order, and carry a nice array of packaged goods from Italy, as well as the typical convenience items and produce. At the cash register, be sure to check out what fruit they are featuring as the day's impulse item for purchase. With possibilities like fragrant Concord grapes, Bing cherries at their peak, or fresh plump figs, their tactic to tempt works every time with me!

Despite its setting among cornfields and orchards, Kemper Lakes is not a sleepy golf course. It's a tough course any way you slice it, so to speak. If you visit in autumn, you'll find conditions that simply increase the level of challenge already present in the course design. Besides an abundance of lakes on the course, a distinguishing feature contributing to the built-in challenge at Kemper is the inclusion of some 60 bowl-shaped bunkers, which make for nearly all downhill lies. Even early on in its existence, Kemper was recognized for its high-caliber play and attractive

scenery. It played host to the PGA Championship in 1989, the year Payne Stewart won. Designed in 1979 by Dick Nugent and Ken Killian, the course features 20 acres of lakes, mature oaks, willows, and pines. The front 9 has a wide-open feel. The lakes are in plain view, and the wind is a real factor. The back 9, by contrast, is heavily treed and features narrower fairways. In fact, the 15th and 16th holes actually parallel each other. The beauty and challenge at Kemper literally builds to a crescendo, making the last five holes particular course highlights.

The need for precise golf starts immediately, and the 3rd hole, which is the shortest on the course, is a little terror. At 112 yards from the white tee, the temptation is to hit the ball too hard to carry it over the water. Anything hit too long that misses the green, however, will instantly be out of bounds. The two-tiered green is made even more difficult by its bell shape, with a mere 20 feet of green on either side.

The next few holes border farmland and old orchards, where corn, blueberries, and apples are still grown, and on the 7th hole, giant willow trees look even more beautiful in their reflected images in the lakes. But the autumn splendor, as bucolic as it may seem, can also wreak havoc on the golf game. For instance, after managing to place my ball safely on the fairway between two fairway bunkers and avoiding the lake that runs left on the par 5 7th hole, the dry fall grass and the sloping grade makes even a layup shot difficult. The drier, faster grass at this time of year makes the ball roll downhill, so any attempt to overcompensate left to avoid the pot bunkers guarding the green at the right could leave you with a ball in the lake. Marshy areas full of cattails await golfers on the 10th hole, making it difficult to find your ball if you err on your drive and play into the rough.

The heavily treed back 9 is gorgeous, with an abundance of so many colors and textures in the fall. Your opening drive on 11 must avoid large oak trees to the left and right of your landing area. The second shot runs through a narrow, treed, downward-sloping corridor. I'm not above resorting to taking punch shots to get out of trouble on this hole or even hitting intentionally into the back bunker and chipping out onto the tiny green.

The finishing holes at Kemper are as challenging as any that I've played. The long par 5 on 15 is truly a three-shot hole. My slightly uphill drive typically has a 260-yard carry, but a stronger drive of 280 yards can catch the roll where the fairway begins to slope downward. Even with a little help, it's another 200 yards to the green. Play it right or the mature trees will block your view to the green.

The 16th hole may be in plain view, but the lake that runs clear along the right of the fairway before wrapping around the green and the scallop-shaped trap behind the green are downright daunting. Take safety by staying in the middle of the fairway. Putting is made difficult by the ridge running through the middle of the green. Once you've gotten over this hurdle, prepare yourself for my nomination for the top par in the country! If you think I'm exaggerating, listen to the experts.

Golf Magazine put Kemper's 17th hole on their recent list of the 500 best holes in the world! The 17th's most distinguishing characteristic is its three-fourths-island green, a peninsula, if you will; and you will need a trip back to The Peninsula Hotel to be soothed and coddled at their spa to recover from this hole! Wind rips at your drive from the big opening of water left, and once you find the green, the challenge only heightens on 17. Its heavily contoured surface is a putting disaster, especially if pin placement is at the back left, nearest to the water. If your ball sinks, it will be in good company. In addition to a few of my balls, it will join many smallmouth bass, which also call the lake "home."

Kemper added three trees to the final hole so that golfers can no longer cut the dogleg to the green like Greg Norman did at the '89 Championship. I hit as close to the lake as I can to avoid the two large bunkers to the right of the landing zone on this hard dogleg left. The second shot must carry over water to a narrow opening leading to the green. It's a tough approach shot, and if you sacrifice a ball to another lake, this time it will live among giant carp! The contoured green keeps you on your toes until the very last shot. I feel pretty lucky to have such a great golf course near me; I hope you'll come to find out for yourself how special Kemper Lakes is.

...I'M EQUALLY CONTENT EXPLORING THE VAST GOLF RESOURCES THAT EXIST IN MY OWN TOWN, CHICAGO.

After a day of golf, I invite you to dine at my restaurant, Pluton. You can tell me how you fared at Kemper! What I strive for at my restaurant is luxurious fine dining that is also comfortable and inviting. I think of Pluton as an extension of my home. To relax my diners into a celebratory state of mind and to keep the atmosphere as far from stuffy as possible, I often incorporate an element of surprise and playfulness into my dishes. Recently, I served a deconstruction of corn chowder to my guests. In addition to kernels of corn, a spoonful of minced black truffles, and some minced chives, my patrons were charmed to find that the soup bowl, into which the creamy soup was poured, contained a small handful of popcorn! My diners really got a kick out of their soup course that night. When I create a dish, I aim to evoke a food memory by making connections for my diners between the seasons and classical favorites. Hopefully, I'll spark some new connections for them as well.

I take a lot of inspiration from Chicago's ethnic neighborhoods, where restaurants serving authentic fare at reasonable prices abound and small-scale grocery stores stock their shelves full of specialty items. For the freshest locally grown and raised organic food, there is no place like Chicago's Green City Market. This outdoor farmer's market, open each Wednesday from 7:00 A.M. to 1:00 P.M., runs from May to October and is located just north of the corner of Clark Street and North Avenue in beautiful Lincoln Park. There's always live music and seating is provided so you can relax and enjoy your cup of coffee or a yogurt smoothie made with seasonal fruit and delicious yogurt from Traderspoint Creamery, located in Zionsville, Indiana. There is also a crepe stand, serving both sweet and savory choices of featured ingredients from the market. I like the Wisconsin maple syrup crepe, a delicious North American twist on the French classic. If you aren't able to follow your nose to locate the crepes, just look for the long line! If it's lunchtime, made-to-order organic burgers are also an option. But I usually grab a baguette from Bennison's Bakery, located in Evanston, Illinois; whatever goat cheese speaks to me from Judith Schad's award-winning Capriole Farms located in Greenville, Indiana; and some local produce. There's nothing like sinking your teeth into a juicy Red Haven peach in the summer or a Honey Crisp apple in the fall, or polishing off a box of berries from Len Klug's farm in Michigan. This man has the touch!

This market really has something for everyone. Each week, the market hosts a chef demonstration at 10:30 A.M., highlighting seasonal foods from the market.

> THE HEAVILY TREED BACK 9 IS GORGEOUS, WITH AN ABUNDANCE OF SO MANY COLORS AND TEXTURES IN THE FALL.

The demonstrations are lively and varied. So much can be found at the Green City Market, including a lot of friendly smiles and knowledgeable purveyors who take real pride in their products and who are happy to share information with visitors to their booths. Stalls are loaded with anything from fresh herbs; local honey; foraged and cultivated mushrooms, available fresh and pickled; seasonal produce, including ethnic and heirloom varieties; canned preserves and tomato products; meat and fish; chicken, duck, and quail eggs; fresh pasta; milk, yogurt, and cheeses; apple cider; breads and tantalizing pastries; not to mention the inedible goodies like plants and flower bouquets. There's even a booth that plies its hand-milled herbal soaps, a handy product after all the feasting that goes on here!

Of course, golf should never be out of the question, and here in Chicago, it's within easy reach. Follow up your visit to the market with a stop at the nearby Diversey Driving Range, open seven days a week year-round; it provides a perfect opportunity for the quick "golf fix"! If you are in the mood to sightsee, I recommend the pleasant $1\frac{1}{2}$-mile walk on the pedestrian trail through the Lincoln Park Zoo from the market to this golf enclave. Hit a couple of buckets of balls in the heated enclosed stalls while looking out to beautiful oaks and willows, with Lake Michigan's sandy beachfront and Diversey Harbor within easy reach. Miniature golf for the junior family members also needing the "golf fix" is right next door!

Or venture just a bit farther north up the lakefront, where at Waveland Avenue you will find the Marovitz Golf Course, a public park-side par-3 course with year-round play, managed by none other than Kemper

Golf Management. Watch the boats sail by while you play for less than 20 dollars a round. The course hugs the lakefront and is sandwiched to the west by Lake Shore Drive. You can't beat the price for this prime real estate! Go the other direction, south of The Magnificent Mile, to Grant Park, and you will find another Chicago treasure, a pristinely manicured miniature golf course. Known as a putting course, there are no props like the kiddie course at Diversey Harbor, just a miniature 18-hole heavily contoured course. Eight dollars buys a round here. If you play here, be sure to visit the outdoor patios at The Green at Grant Park. The café looks out to the putting course and serves refreshing drinks, like sangria, to complement its upscale bar fare, like the surf and turf club, a sandwich of lobster meat and cold beef tenderloin, chunky gazpacho soup, and quesadillas. A great destination for a laid-back Sunday brunch, The Green is even better on a warm evening, when the lights of Michigan Avenue and the colorful splendor of Buckingham Fountain are visible in the distance.

For those whose idea of hitting the links is more akin to sinking their teeth into a Polish sausage than playing a round of golf, my friend and fellow Chicagoan, Evelyn Thompson, can answer that call. Since 1981, Evelyn has been leading small groups on food-related tours of Chicago's ethnic neighborhoods. Her knowledge is expansive, and she can organize a tour to cover almost any ethnic neighborhood in the city. Tap into Chicago's Jamaican resources with her, explore Chinatown, or check out a Mexican neighborhood in Pilsen. Or head to Chicago's north side with Evelyn to experience neighborhood options that include Cuban, East African, Middle Eastern, Bosnian, Indian, Russian, Vietnamese, and Thai.

The day Evelyn and I met to explore Chicago's Polish neighborhood in Avondale on North Milwaukee Avenue, Evelyn, always well prepared, came armed with enticing recipes and fact books, as well as an itinerary for our walking tour through the neighborhood's many bakeries, general stores, and sausage shops.

She recommends shopping at the markets when it's not busy so there will be greater opportunity to stop and chat with people. Even if the butchers don't understand you, she says, the customers standing behind you will. It's a great way to ask questions and get recipe ideas. We made our first stop at Stanley's Sausage Shop on Belmont Avenue, an old-school store that still makes its own sausages. We sampled a slice of a few smoked meats before moving on to Milwaukee Avenue, otherwise known as the Honorary Polish Village. Evelyn supplied me with the interesting fact that Chicago actually boasts the world's largest Polish population outside of Poland and proudly celebrates Casimir Pulaski Day each year in March, for which nearby Pulaski Avenue is named.

> CHICAGO ACTUALLY BOASTS THE WORLD'S LARGEST POLISH POPULATION OUTSIDE OF POLAND.

Once on Milwaukee Avenue, we entered Wally's Market, a supermarket on a grand scale, catering to the modern shopper who wants the ability to buy all of the traditional Polish foods with the convenience of free parking. Wally's bakery section greets you upon entering. I happily munched on some herbatniki, which are poppy seed tea cookies, while I perused the aisles and peeked into huge kraut and pickle barrels. Like all of the sausage shops in the neighborhood, the walls of Wally's deli section are lined with dozens of sausages, some smoked, some baked, and some made with garlic. And like Chicago's wide range in golf course options, there is tremendous variation in these links as well; you'll find sausages made with chicken, beef, or pork. A skinny variety that I was happy to discover, called "kabonos," is eaten at room temperature as a snack. I grabbed a rope to munch on later and then continued my walking tour with Evelyn. We poked into a few of the herbalist shops and more delis and bakeries before breaking for lunch.

We headed to Angelica's, where we filled up on crispy potato pancakes smothered with a rich mushroom sauce and bowls of red beet borscht. This hot and sturdy soup full of chunks of carrots, potatoes, and hard-cooked eggs was enhanced by a generous sprinkle of chopped fresh dill weed, the classic garnish to Polish food. Like our lunch combination, eating at Angelica's can only be described as a win-win situation. The food is a sure

CHICAGO IS ALWAYS GOING THAT EXTRA MILE.

bet, and the service is always friendly. Little square crepes filled with sweet cheese, called "nalesniki z serem," which I had purchased earlier in the day from Wally's made a great ending to a delicious meal. My belly was full, yet there was barely a dent in my wallet, so Evelyn and I made one last stop at Pasieka Bakery for a fresh loaf of rye bread. Evelyn is a real pro in her field of work, and spending a day with her touring an ethnic neighborhood really allows me to discover new foods and new places. I find that these experiences spark inventiveness in my own cooking and help to keep me at the top of my game.

Whether you confine yourself to a small area of Chicago or branch out to explore its many neighborhoods and suburbs, you will find great golf opportunities and enriching experiences. The spirit of joie de vivre is very much a part of Chicago and its environs, and far from what has often been described as a second-city image, Chicago is leading the way in North America in the hotel and hospitality industry. We're not resting on any laurels here; Chicago is always going that extra mile to achieve greatness, and Chicago is a place I proudly call home. Experience for yourself all that this great city has to offer. Check out all of the peninsulas in Chicago, from the formidable hotel on the Magnificent Mile to Kemper's signature hole 17 and all of the other food and golfing highlights in between. Now, if we could only get the Cubs to win the World Series!

ONION SOUP

RATING: A Long Par 4; Low Greens Fees

SERVES: 8

Onion soup is a delicious and hearty first course. By properly caramelizing the onions, you will succeed in transforming them from their raw and biting state to a relaxed and sweet one, and your soup will have an unparalleled depth of flavor. Some may think of this as classic French onion soup, but I think it is Chicago, through and through.

Soup
1 (1 pound) block Parmesan cheese
8 to 10 large onions
olive oil
1 cup white wine
salt and freshly ground pepper to taste
1 bay leaf
8 whole peppercorns
3 quarts Veal Stock (page 180)
1 ounce (2 tablespoons) brandy

Croutons
1 baguette
2 or 3 garlic cloves
olive oil
salt and freshly ground pepper to taste

For the soup, cut the rind from the Parmesan cheese and reserve for the onion stock; shred the remaining cheese and reserve for finishing the soup. Cut the tops and bottoms from the onions and reserve for the onion stock. Peel the onions and slice thinly.

Heat a large sauté pan until smoking. Add 1 tablespoon olive oil and just enough sliced onions at a time to cover the pan in a single layer; do not overload the pan or the onions will steam instead of caramelize. Sauté until the onions are caramelized to a deep golden brown.

Add some of the white wine to deglaze the pan, scraping up any browned bits with a wooden spoon. Remove to a storage container and season with salt and pepper. Repeat the process with the remaining onions and wine.

Combine the reserved Parmesan rind, bay leaf and peppercorns in a cheesecloth sachet. Combine the sachet with the Veal Stock and the reserved onion tops and bottoms in a large stockpot. Bring to a boil and reduce the heat; simmer for 45 minutes or longer if a more strongly flavored soup base is preferred.

Strain the onion stock, discarding the sachet. Return the stock to the stockpot and add the onions and brandy. Simmer for 20 minutes longer. Season with salt and pepper to taste.

For the croutons, preheat the oven to 400 degrees. Slice the baguette diagonally into 1/2-inch-thick slices. Cut off the tops of the garlic cloves, exposing the juices, and rub the cut sides against both sides of the bread slices. Brush both sides of the bread with olive oil and season with salt and pepper. Arrange on a baking sheet and bake until crunchy.

To serve, ladle the soup into heavy ceramic or earthenware soup bowls, filling each 3/4 full. Top each bowl with 2 or 3 of the croutons and sprinkle with the reserved shredded Parmesan cheese. Broil or microwave until the cheese melts and serve immediately.

TIP: To prevent the sachet from sticking to the bottom of the stockpot and burning, tie it with a long piece of butcher's twine and tie the other end to the handle of the stockpot.

SHREDDED PORK SHOULDER ON ONION BUNS

RATING: A Long Par 4; Average Greens Fees

SERVES: A Crowd

After an early morning of golf, invite the gang back to your house for a stick-to-your-ribs lunch. Prepare the filling the day before so that your hungry crowd can assemble their sandwich, take a scoop of potato salad and eat right away.

4 pounds boneless pork
   shoulder, trimmed of
   excess fat
salt and freshly ground
   pepper to taste
1/2 carrot
1/2 rib celery
1/2 onion
salt and freshly ground
   pepper to taste
1 bay leaf
1 quart Chicken Stock
   (page 179)
1/4 cup mayonnaise
2 tablespoons chopped
   parsley
onion buns
arugula, spinach or
   lettuce leaves
1 or 2 tomatoes, sliced

Preheat the oven to 350 degrees. Season the pork shoulder generously with salt and pepper. Sear the pork in a deep roasting pan until golden brown on all sides. Remove to a plate.

Add the carrot, celery and onion to the roasting pan; season with salt and pepper and add the bay leaf. Cook until caramelized. Drain any excess drippings from the pan and return the pork and any accumulated juices to the pan. Add enough Chicken Stock to cover the pork.

Roast, covered, for about 1 1/2 hours or until very tender, turning the pork every 15 minutes so that it will cook evenly. Remove the pork, carrot, onion, celery and bay leaf from the pan, reserving the stock in the pan. Let the pork stand until cool enough to handle and shred.

Cook the reserved stock over high heat until reduced to a glaze. Let stand until cool, then whisk in the mayonnaise and parsley.

Warm or grill the buns. Spread with the mayonnaise mixture, add your leaves of choice and sliced tomatoes and top with the shredded meat. Serve cold, warmed or piping hot.

TIP: The crispy onions from the accompanying Cold Potato Salad recipe (page 24) are great on this sandwich!

COLD POTATO SALAD

RATING: A Long Par 3; Average Greens Fees

SERVES: 6 to 8

What's a casual lunch buffet without potato salad, especially when taking inspiration from the meat and potatoes capital! Like the accompanying shredded pork sandwich, this dish can mostly be made ahead of time.

4 large Idaho potatoes
1 sprig rosemary
1 sprig thyme
1 head garlic, cut into halves crosswise
1 bay leaf
2 tablespoons chopped chives
2 tablespoons finely chopped shallots
6 tablespoons Mustard Dressing (page 176)
1 medium red onion
1 cup flour
3 to 4 cups vegetable oil
salt and freshly ground pepper to taste
8 slices bacon, crisp-cooked and crumbled

Preheat the oven to 350 degrees. Place the potatoes on a large sheet of heavy foil and add the rosemary, thyme, garlic and bay leaf. Wrap the foil to enclose the potatoes and poke several holes in the foil to allow steam to escape. Bake for about 1 hour and 20 minutes; do not overbake or the potatoes will fall apart in the salad.

Remove the potatoes from the foil, discarding the foil and herbs. Let stand until cool and cut into medium pieces. Combine with the chives and shallots in a bowl. Add the Mustard Dressing and mix gently. Chill in the refrigerator.

Slice the onion very thin and separate into rings. Dust with the flour. Fill a large saucepan halfway with vegetable oil and heat to 300 degrees. Add the onions and deep-fry until crisp. Remove to drain on paper towels and season with salt and pepper.

Just before serving, adjust the seasoning in the salad and fold in the crumbled bacon. Top with the fried onions.

TIP: If you prefer a stronger bacon flavor, reserve the drippings from frying the bacon and fold them into the salad.

OVEN-BAKED WHITEFISH WITH CARAMELIZED RED ONIONS

RATING: Par for the Course on a Par 3; Average Greens Fees

SERVES: 4

Mild whitefish from the waters of Lake Michigan is a favorite of many of my bistro customers in Chicago, and onions and the Chicago area, believe it or not, have gone hand in hand for centuries. Chicago derives its name from the Native Americans' description of the area as the "stinking onion." In this dish, neither the fish nor the onions are strong or stinky. The super sweet red onions bathe the delicate fish in gentle but rich flavor.

6 tablespoons olive oil
2 tablespoons butter
1 tablespoon sugar
2 medium red onions, sliced 1/4 inch thick
2 tablespoons butter
salt and freshly ground pepper to taste
2 tablespoons red wine vinegar
4 fresh whitefish fillets with the skin

Preheat the oven to 475 degrees. Heat a large sauté pan and add the olive oil and 2 tablespoons butter. Sprinkle the sugar evenly in the pan. Add the onion slices without crowding the pan and sear on both sides to caramelize; crowding the slices will cause them to steam instead of brown.

Arrange the onions in a 9×11-inch baking dish and dot with 2 tablespoons butter. Season with salt and pepper and drizzle with the vinegar. Season the fish fillets with salt and pepper and arrange them skin side up on the onions.

Cover the dish with foil and bake for about 11 minutes or until the fillets are opaque but still somewhat firm.

TIP: Select fillets of the same size to ensure even cooking, and to keep your guests from arguing over who got the biggest portion of delicious whitefish!

CORN FLAN

RATING: A Short Par 3; Low Greens Fees

SERVES: 6 to 8

Bring the flavors of a Midwest corn harvest to your table anytime. If fresh corn on the cob is not in season, canned or frozen corn will work as a fine substitute.

5 eggs
1 cup creamed corn
1/2 cup corn kernels
1 cup heavy cream
salt and freshly ground pepper to taste
2 tablespoons chopped chives, for garnish

Preheat the oven to 350 degrees. Whisk the eggs, creamed corn and corn kernels together in a bowl. Whisk the cream gradually into the mixture and season to taste with salt and pepper.

Fill ramekins 2/3 full with the corn mixture and place them in a baking pan. Pour boiling water to a depth of 1 inch in the baking pan. Cover with foil and bake for 35 minutes.

Run a knife around the inside of each ramekin and invert onto plates, or serve in the individual ramekins. Garnish with the chopped chives.

Warm Strawberries with Raspberry Wine

RATING: A Short Par 3; High Greens Fees

SERVES: 4

The Glunz Family Winery & Cellars in Grayslake, Illinois, makes their raspberry wine from raspberries grown on the Glunz family farm. When I play Kemper Lakes, I have a built-in excuse to swing by the winery to stock up my inventory—I'm in the neighborhood! Another opportunity to enjoy the Glunz's wine is at Christmas time, when Chicago hosts the annual Christkindlmarket at the Daley Center Plaza downtown, and the Glunz family serves its hot spiced wine, called Glug. The family also owns the oldest wine and spirits retail store, located in Old Town at Division and Wells streets near my restaurant, Pluton. Be sure to take a bottle of their raspberry wine home with you the next time you visit Chicago. This dish is the perfect impromptu, but elegant, dessert.

1 1/2 pints strawberries
2 tablespoons butter
1 tablespoon sugar
1/2 cup raspberry wine
freshly ground pepper to taste

Remove the stems and leaves from the strawberries and cut them into quarters; pat completely dry. Heat the butter in a saucepan and add the strawberries. Sauté for several minutes. Add the sugar and sauté until the strawberries begin to release their juice.

Add the wine and stir to deglaze the pan. Cook until most of the alcohol in the wine has evaporated. Season with pepper to serve.

TIP: Wash the strawberries with the stems and leaves attached. This helps to prevent the berries from absorbing water.

My passion for golf amounts to true reverence when it comes to playing

at Pebble Beach on California's Monterey Peninsula.

My three must-play courses equate to my golfing version of a holy trinity. The famed Pebble Beach Golf Links Course, currently ranked the number one public course by *Golf Digest* and *Golf Magazine*, has played host to four memorable U.S. Open Championships and the star-studded National Pro-Am tournament, where golf history has solidified into the stuff of legend. Nearby, Spyglass Hill Golf Course features treacherous golf that is divided between stunning ocean and forest settings. The Links at Spanish Bay may be the area's newest golf course, but its strong resemblance to traditional Scottish links, down to the evening bagpiper who signals the end of each day's play, makes this a course not to be forgotten.

When I visited, I wound my way to Pebble Beach through a stretch of road called 17-mile Drive, which hugs the Pacific Ocean and delivers one striking view after another. The private road, accessible by any one of the five gated entrances, is part of the property held by Pebble Beach Resorts. It was June, and though it would have been more typical to have a foggy day on the Peninsula, I was met with a day full of sunshine, brightening my already high spirits. I headed directly to The Lodge, the resort's original hotel, as I was eager for a first glimpse of the Pebble Beach Golf Links Course.

A GOLFING PILGRIMAGE

PEBBLE

BEACH

California's Monterey Peninsula

Pebble Beach Golf Links, a public
course since its opening in 1919,
plays host to the dream games
of over 50,000 golfers each year

This is a breathtaking...

Sparkling in the afternoon light, there was the first tee at Pebble Beach. So many great moments in golf have taken place right on this course. Stepping onto the grass felt like walking on hallowed ground. Part of Pebble Beach's mystique stems from the fact that it has remained a public golf course since its unveiling in 1919; and because of this, it embodies the qualities of the American Dream. Though a round of golf at Pebble Beach may set you back more than most, it is open to anyone who wants to play. As a fellow golfer put it as he called out a greeting to me the first day I played the course, he's living the dream! And you can, too! More than 50,000 golfers of all levels of play come to play Pebble each year, which is a testament not only to how revered the course has become but also to its incredibly high level of maintenance. This is no exclusive, private club where a few thousand rounds are played each year, but rather here is a place where it is possible for literally anyone to have the experience of playing an elite course and attempt to achieve the near impossible.

Where else but at Pebble Beach would a grandfather come out of retirement to win a third National Pro-Am title? Johnny Miller did just that in 1994, capping off wins in three decades of play, also winning the 1974 and 1987 competitions here. Exciting things always seem to happen at Pebble Beach, like at the first U.S. Open held here in 1972, when Jack Nicklaus put the ball on the beach on the 10th hole, recovered, and then hit the flagstick at 17 and won the tournament. Tournament play at Pebble has always produced memorable moments, and they couldn't have scripted

a better tournament than the 2000 U.S. Open, when Tiger Woods finished 12 under par.

Pebble Beach's draw reaches far beyond the professional golf tour. The sixth fairway provided the setting for the 1945 movie *National Velvet*, which starred Elizabeth Taylor and Mickey Rooney. In fact, the resort has a long-standing history of hosting big names from Hollywood and other celebrities who have attended seasonal events like horse shows, equestrian competitions, and car shows, or played in the Bing Crosby, now the AT&T, National Pro-Am every winter.

The severe conditions that have often plagued the Pro-Am competition over the years have been fondly dubbed "Crosby weather." Shortly before a Pro-Am tournament was scheduled to begin several years ago, the aftermath of a wicked storm left the course covered with standing pools of water. It looked like another cancellation was inevitable, but once again Pebble Beach proved that here the impossible is possible. Clint Eastwood and John Denver simply hovered above the course in a helicopter and blew the water right off the course!

For me, Pebble Beach's dramatic history makes me both nervous and excited. I've long harbored a secret fantasy of nailing a personal best here. I upped my chances of making this dream a reality by playing the course not once but twice. I treated my first round as the warm-up; I took in the lay of the land—a luxury enjoyed by the pros, which pays big dividends when it counts during tournament play—and tried to harness my awestruck mind-set to get ready for a second, more-focused round of golf at the Pebble Beach Golf Links.

During my first round of play, I couldn't help noticing the small greens on this course. Apparently, when it opened in 1919, Pebble Beach represented an advancement for its time in golf landscape design by building irrigation systems into the tees and greens. Prior to this, it was difficult to maintain greens on California courses; many could easily have been called *browns*, as they were essentially made from oil-packed sand. Though the irrigation infrastructure was in place from day one and the nearby military corps obliged by hauling tons of horse fertilizer over to the course to get the soil up to grass-growing standard, maintenance capabilities dictated the petite size of the greens. Now they are one of Pebble Beach's defining attributes.

One of the only significant changes made since the course opened for play in 1919 was actually part of the original vision of its founder, Samuel F. B. Morse, but remained unrealized until 1998, when Jack Nicklaus helped replace the old dogleg par 3 on the 5th hole. Where it had turned inland, the newly positioned tee box is now aligned with the green and fits naturally along the ocean bluffs. It makes for a picture-perfect shot on calm days. However, when wind factors into play, even the pros have trouble making par.

On number 6, a par 5, I recalled how Tiger Woods, appearing to be in trouble in the rough, used a 7-iron to hit his ball uphill over an oak tree and right onto the green. That was one of the classic moments of the 2000 U.S. Open. Some other classic moments and not so classic moments in Pebble's history occurred on the 10th.

The white sandy beaches below would be more precise. Here is where the likes of Jack Nicklaus and Arnold Palmer have played out. The beach there is considered fair territory as long as you don't ground your club. Ray Romano also found himself flailing in golf purgatory on the beach during a celebrity Pro-Am. He is a heck of a comedian; maybe he was just clowning, but I don't think he fared too well that day.

It wasn't whale season, but I did spot some sea otters sunning themselves on the rocks and a lot of beautiful birds in flight. In addition to all the famous personalities who have played Pebble, the animal and natural wildlife should get equal billing. This is a breathtaking piece of the world. With one round under my belt, I gained some confidence and felt able to turn my attention temporarily away from Pebble golf to the other wonderful things on the Monterey Peninsula.

Pebble Beach was voted Best Golf Resort in the 2003 *Travel & Leisure* "World's Best Golf Resorts Reader's Survey." You can't go wrong with any of the resort's three lodging options. The Lodge is the resort's original facility and exudes classic charm. With rooms looking out to the Pebble Beach Golf Links, the main building is just west of the Beach & Tennis Club. As a guest of the resort, you are welcome to relax by the club's terraced pool with its oceanfront setting and enjoy lunch at the Beach Club dining room, a grand salon with panoramic views of Carmel Bay.

...piece of the world.

Luxurious rooms and the old-world elegance of an Italian villa, complete with trellised walkways, gently gurgling fountains, and cascading potted flowers at every turn, offer a serene respite at Casa Palmero, the resort's newest boutique hotel, situated along Pebble's first two fairways.

Tiger likes to stay here. Heading north along 17-Mile Drive, about four miles from the town of Monterey, is The Inn at Spanish Bay, the third hotel comprising the Pebble Beach Resort complex. Set among Monterey pines, the hotel is a gateway to more than 34 miles of scenic trails that weave through the Del Monte Forest and white sandy beaches of the Pacific Ocean shoreline.

The resort's dining options not only feature stellar food, much of which is prepared with local seafood and regional produce; the restaurants also offer tantalizing views of the golf courses set amidst the peninsula's rugged natural beauty. To cap off my first day at Pebble Beach, I chose a front-row seat to Pebble Beach's 18th green with Carmel Bay visible in the distance at Club XIX, the resort's premier dining room. While enjoying the sunset and the chef's *amuse-bouche* of a single raw oyster topped with matchsticks of crunchy radish and a spoonful of caviar that was presented in a gentle bath of pea soup, I relished another of Pebble Beach's delightful moments.

I decided on the locally farmed abalone to follow an artfully presented and perfectly prepared first course of sea scallops. The napoleon of sautéed abalone and candied disks of daikon radish with sea urchin fondue was outstanding. The dish's sweeter flavors and delicate textures were balanced by the toothsome and meaty shellfish, the rich and almost nutty qualities of the sea urchin sauce and the earthiness of the salsify and shiitake mushrooms that rounded out the complex entrée. Having enjoyed the abalone dish so much, I was really glad to learn that the once-threatened abalone is rebounding and being farmed here with the aid and guidance of the Monterey Bay Aquarium. The local sardine population, once a thriving local industry captured by John Steinbeck in his novel *Cannery Row*, has been decimated over the years; I was intrigued by the aquarium's push to revitalize this endangered food, too. Over dessert, I decided that a visit to the Monterey Bay Aquarium was a must.

Just a 20-minute drive from Pebble Beach, I made my way through the low, silvery morning light and arrived at the aquarium located right on historic Cannery Row. It is the largest marine sanctuary in the country, and its presence on the peninsula truly builds upon the area's colorful past by impacting strongly and positively on Monterey's present-day environment. Among the aquarium's amazing displays is a three-story living kelp forest which, I am happy to report, many schools of sardines can again call their home. There is also a jellyfish gallery and a sort of aquatic petting zoo of sharks and rays. There are many other attractions on Cannery Row, ranging from a 19th-century carousel to a wine-tasting center that features regional wines. But golf was calling me back to Pebble Beach. I needed to get back for my afternoon tee time at the Links at Spanish Bay.

I met up with Head Golf Pro Rich Cosand, who is extremely knowledgeable about both the area and the course itself. He explained that Spanish Bay was the actual site at Monterey where the Spanish conquistadors landed in the 1500s. I mentioned my recent visit to the Monterey Bay Aquarium and that I learned Spanish Bay was once a Native American sacred cooking site, evidenced by the countless stacks of abalone shells that have been unearthed from the sand. Rich also explained that the course is home to wetlands preserves. If you hit a ball into any of these environmentally sensitive areas, local rules state that you cannot play out. Drops are allowed outside of these areas and a penalty stroke is charged. Other unique features of the course are the ocean views

He said that here, more than any other hole, is where you get into trouble and add to your score. On 9, for instance, the entire right side is out of bounds. Putting on this hole also gave me some pause. Rich helpfully pointed out that the predominant break to the grass is always toward the ocean. Knowing this helped me make a better read, and I managed par.

The double-dogleg par 5 on the next hole features an uphill elevation before a series of bunkers. For my second shot, I decided to play it short with a 5-iron to avoid the pot bunkers, leaving only 100 yards to the pin. The hump in the middle of the green creates a unique tiered effect. I liked 11, as it presented so many options. Because of the downward-sloping approach to the green, I chose to avoid the front edge and the

He explained that Spanish Bay was the actual site at Monterey where the Spanish conquistadors landed in the 1500s.

from every hole. From hole 6, don't miss the lookout to Point Joe, known as the restless sea. This is the meeting point of the Pacific and Japanese currents.

The course opened in 1988. Tom Watson, who together with Robert Trent Jones, Jr., and Sandy Tatum designed the Links at Spanish Bay, holds the course record, a 67. As Rich and I made our way through the front 9, I noticed that there are not a lot of flat lies on this course with its heavy undulations, but the wetlands preserve on holes 7, 8 and 9 proved to be the most challenging obstacle yet. On the 8th, I had to navigate over about a 160-yard wetlands pond before finding the narrow green. The wind coming off the water only further complicated things. Though a real risk-and-reward course, Rich cautioned me about these wetlands holes.

wind that was starting to pick up by using low, running shots. Hole 12, by contrast, demands a lot of ball carry, over a canyon to an elevated green. The narrow fairway on this hole, with its dense border of immense trees, is a bit of an anomaly for a links course.

Thirteen was most definitely not my lucky number. The sea breezes wreaked havoc on my accuracy. Rich described the green as a postage stamp, and my lack of touch resulted in a very late delivery, more like return to sender! I ended up with a triple bogey on this small but mighty 99-yard par 3. Rich sensed my mounting frustration and cautioned against using my driver on 14. With the afternoon sea breezes in effect, compounded by the risk of slicing into some trees, Rich suggested a 3-wood to stay in play. His advice proved valuable on the next hole as well.

From the tee box, the fairway looks really tight, but Rich assured me that it is actually a landing area of generous size. Sometimes, you just have to place your trust with the expert. Once clear of the dune and onto the green, I was able to regroup. I think the 17th hole is my personal favorite at Spanish Bay. I teed off into a majestic ocean view. The sound of waves and the smell of ocean air were reinvigorating. From the tee box, there doesn't seem to be much of a target, but I had the success of dealing with a similar situation on 15 under my belt, so I stepped up to the challenge of a massive first shot. Sure enough, once on the fairway, there was plenty of room to avoid the deep pot bunkers on the right. I finished the round much obliged to Rich's ability to read the course and my game.

As we left the course, sounds of the evening bagpiper filled the air. I found a comfortable chair on the terrace of Roy's overlooking the course, ordered a glass of chardonnay from Monterey County, and took in the very Scottish ambience.

There is nothing Scottish about Spyglass, though it is a tough course in a rugged sort of way. Robert Trent Jones, Sr., modeled the first five holes after Pine Valley, emphasizing the land's natural features of ocean and sand dunes. The balance of the course is forested, with the last five holes in homage to Augusta National. It is believed that Robert Louis Stevenson roamed the area and found inspiration here for his classic pirate adventure novel *Treasure Island*, which he wrote in 1883.

> AS WE LEFT THE COURSE, SOUNDS OF THE EVENING BAGPIPER FILLED THE AIR.

Naming the course after the novel and playing off *Treasure Island*'s story line, Jones named the holes after characters and places in the novel with similar attributes. Spyglass's head golf pro, Bill Sendell, a guy who never wears a watch because he has an uncanny ability to tell time by gut instinct, most definitely has a bit of the pirate spirit. He challenges any first-timers to Spyglass to finish better than ten shots over their handicap.

I was willing to take up his challenge but ended up walking the proverbial plank. Ranked number five last year on *Golf Digest*'s list of 100 Greatest American Courses, this course forces golfers to flirt with danger nearly every step of the way. I have to admit that it was the most fun I've had getting into and trying to get out of golf trouble.

Jones's design consistently creates danger in the front of the green by utilizing uphill features. At 6,114 yards from the white tees, the uphill shots make the course play longer. Seldom will golfers find their ball on even ground. This holds true on the fairways and in the rough. The ice plant that covers much of the dunes around the first five holes is a sort of botanical siren, beautiful in its unusual mahogany allure but deadly if you fall into its clutches. A member of the succulent family, this indigenous plant will actually act as a tee if your ball happens to sit on top of it! Should you find that your ball gets caught among this ground cover like mine did, though, you'll find it to be unplayable. Such was my experience on my opening shot. By the 4th hole, I was well on my way to losing my bet with Bill. This hole's name, "Blind Pew," refers to its blind tee shot. To make matters worse, the farther you hit the ball, the narrower the fairway. With ice plant surrounding the green, this par 4 about did me in! Spyglass's most difficult hole, number eight, is the longest par 4 I have ever played. It's not the hole's actual distance, at 354 yards from the white tee, that is the cause; it's the steep uphill fairway sloping left to right and leading to the elevated, downward-sloped green with a bunker protecting it on the right.

By this point in our round, I was resigned to enjoying the course's beauty and getting out of there alive. The necklace of bunkers around the green on 11 was quite picturesque at a distance, but once again I found myself in its clutches. Getting out of this trap was tricky at best. I think at this point, Bill began to take pity on me. He recommended a 7-iron on my short approach shot at 14. Pin placement was in front, but I needed the extra club to contend with the swirling wind. By the end of the round, I had literally used every club. Spyglass is not a course to be taken lightly. It might be the ultimate in humbling courses. In fact, it consistently posts the highest scores on the Pro-Am. Glad to know I'm in good company!

Though I had had a humbling morning on the golf course, I still had the rest of the day to sink my teeth into exploring the area. As it was time for lunch, I headed over to Stillwater Bar & Grill at the Lodge, where Executive Chef Jeff Jake joined me. Our table in the airy room looked right out to the 18th of the Pebble Beach Golf Links and the white, sandy beaches of Carmel Bay and Stillwater Cove. Jake's cooking style is an outgrowth of California cuisine, a movement that focuses on locally, organically raised food. From his early days cooking in the Napa Valley thirty years ago, Chef Jake developed a reverence for his area's food and its flavor profiles that are specific to the land in which it is grown.

A chef who understands *terroir*, the soul of the soil, is a chef who gets everything out of food and brings delicious, but oftentimes elusive, flavors to the table. With that said, there's no wonder Stillwater is considered the finest Sunday buffet brunch on the peninsula. The summer menu reflects local, seasonal ingredients like sand dabs, calamari, and wild salmon, as well as a lush assortment of local berries, artichokes, and mushrooms. Chef Jake recommended Talbot, a local sauvignon blanc, to accompany our lunch.

We began with sashimi of yellowtail, simply dressed with a lemon-infused olive oil. Commenting on how much I enjoyed the delicate pairing, Chef Jake shared one kitchen secret with me. The olive oil he uses comes from his sister's operation in Napa—the St. Helena Olive Oil Company. I had recently been to her retail store while in Napa Valley and lamented the fact that although I made a number of purchases there, I did not buy any of the lemon-infused olive oil. The chef excused himself for a moment, returning with a souvenir for me; his gracious gift contained a bottle of the lemon oil and a cap embroidered with the Pebble Beach logo. Here was yet another instance where the marriage of golf and food produces a winning combination. Chef Jake is a most generous host and truly a gifted chef.

We then feasted on fritters of local sand dabs and French fries, accompanied by a multi-colored cabbage slaw. The slaw's mayonnaise-based dressing was all I needed for dipping my crunchy fish and chips, Monterey-style. We passed an enjoyable afternoon, talking of our passions, namely food and golf. He fully appreciated my delight at spotting a huge clump of wild fennel growing near the 8th tee box at Pebble a few days earlier. Speaking of *terroir*, that's some pretty impressive farm real estate! Thinking of that first round there and the challenges I had been up against at Spanish Bay and Spyglass, I felt like I was indeed due for a solid round of golf. I was full and content from my delicious lunch and the chef's good company, so I was in just the right frame of mind to begin mentally preparing for my second round at the Pebble Beach Golf Links.

My final day at Pebble Beach didn't amount to Crosby weather, but it was thick with fog. Rather than viewing this as a drawback, I took it as a lucky sign. I always play better in Scottish weather. Maybe it's the lack of distraction, but I tend to focus and concentrate on my game in the dense, cool air. There was virtually no wind to blow the fog out and the cool temps showed no sign that the fog would burn off. This was my kind of day!

I was off to a good start and decided to play the 2nd hole conservatively. I remembered the deep sand gully about 75 yards from the green, so I laid up short on my second shot with a 7-iron and had an easy pitch onto the green. Rich Cosand's tip at Spanish Bay—that the nap of the grass grows in the direction of the ocean— helped me read the break of the green.

I passed Stillwater Cove on my way to tee off at the 4th hole. Holes 4 through 10 hug the ocean, but because of the foggy conditions, distracting beautiful ocean vistas were no longer a factor in my game. On 5, I thanked the golfing gods that there was no wind, and I nailed it for par. On 7, the fog was so dense that

I couldn't make out the green. With conditions as such, the short and formerly benign par 3, with its green well guarded by sand traps, became a bit of a menace. I got into trouble and had to grab for my sand wedge.

When I teed off at number 8, I kept my ball left, well away from the steep cliff on the right. My second shot was a good 190 yards out. Jack Nicklaus has called this hole the greatest second shot in all of golf. With visibility low, I did not want to try a duplication of Nicklaus' shot over the mighty chasm. It was not worth the risk of losing my ball to the great void and ocean way below, not when the stakes I had set for myself were so high. I was going for a personal best here, and not even the greatest second shot in golf could make me lose focus. I hugged the left side of the fairway, navigated the bunkers and contended with the difficult green. It slopes downward from the back to the front. It wasn't pretty; I bogeyed the hole, but I kept my ball.

I stayed clear of the ocean on 9 and 10, and then headed away from the ocean-side holes. In fact, I fared better on the next few holes, despite their faster greens. At 14, I had to regroup somewhat. At 545 yards, the dogleg right par 5 demands a lot of club and carry. After so much intense golf the last couple of days, I was beginning to feel signs of fatigue. When I got to the green, I had the sense that the round was almost over. My realization was bittersweet. Though I was anxious to finish the round with one of my top scores, I was reluctant to say good-bye to Pebble and my time here. It felt like I had just a few bites of a favorite dish left on my plate, a dish that might be the best one I had ever eaten. It would be a pity when the meal was over, but I couldn't suspend time either. I savored the last few holes at Pebble, like the delectable last golf morsels

that they were, swallowed them down, and then committed them to memory for all time.

So onward I pressed. I was careful to avoid the cluster of oaks on 15. My well-placed drive set me up for a short-iron to the green. Unfortunately, by 17, things started to get away from me, as the fog was beginning to lift. I could see the ocean behind the green and began to lose my composure once thoughts of Pebble Beach's long history and mystique started to swirl around in my head again. Now the weather was fine and my thoughts were clouding. With the distracting ocean view, I lost the rhythm of my game and essentially choked on the last two holes. Maybe I should have left the last proverbial golf bites on my plate after all! I did not shoot my personal best at Pebble, but I had a fantastic time making the attempt. Who knows, maybe I'll best myself here the next time I play the course.

In any case, I left Pebble Beach golf behind me and headed over to the spa to recover from four exhausting rounds of play. The spa features a thematic selection of services inspired from the Monterey Peninsula, ranging from water-based services that emphasize the use of seaweed and sea salts to forest-based services. These include a warm pebble massage, an evergreen exfoliation, a wild strawberry scrub, and a rosemary microderm body treatment.

Of course, I homed right in on the golfer's spa services, opting first for the "Chocolate Float." Submerged in a dry, heated flotation bed for 45 minutes, I woke from my much-needed nap to a chocolate smoothie. It was the perfect form of relaxation and refreshment before a 50-minute post-golf therapy massage, followed by a 25-minute foot soother. As a final spa service, I encourage everyone to indulge in the Pebble Beach Water Experience by beginning with the golfer's soak. Then step into a steam, sauna, or inhalation room before showering off in one of the spa's signature showers, featuring colorful ceramic oceanic relief tiles and sixteen body jets that simultaneously kick out cold and hot water while an overhead waterfall cascades down your tired golfer's shoulders.

After such a psychic rush of excitement and adrenaline for the past few days experiencing all that Pebble Beach has to offer, the time I spent at the spa was more than just a cleansing process. It also washed away my aches and pains and left me feeling peaceful. Golf at Pebble Beach had most definitely exceeded my expectations. Pebble Beach's trinity of golf courses does indeed include a father, a son, and a holy spirit, or spirits. Robert Trent Jones, Sr.'s, Spyglass is the ultimate in rugged adventure, while his son's Spanish Bay features all the ingredients of a classic Scottish links course, down to the bagpiper. The spirit of legendary golf for the professional and amateur alike is very much alive at Pebble Beach Golf Links. You feel it on this intimate course, linked together by its diminutive tee boxes and greens, when a fierce breeze off the ocean blows at you or while standing in the thickness of a summer fog. The spirit of golf at Pebble is forever in all of us.

THREE CHEESE "TEE" SANDWICHES

RATING: A Short Par 3; Average Greens Fees
SERVES: A Crowd

These three versions of finger sandwiches transform the tired tea sandwich into tasty and interesting "tee" sandwiches! Guests will be delighted by the delicious bites, and as will the cook by their simple preparation. "Tee" sandwiches make great appetizers as well as a natural pairing for soup to create a light meal.

Goat Cheese Hoagie
4 (4-inch) miniature French loaves
8 ounces sharp goat cheese, cut into 4 pieces
4 romaine leaves, trimmed
1 plum tomato, cut into 8 slices

Monterey Jack Grilled Cheese
4 (1 1/2-ounce) slices Monterey Jack cheese
8 slices of brioche or challah
salt and freshly ground pepper to taste
1/4 cup (1/2 stick) butter

Mini Brie Sandwiches
8 slices of brioche or challah
2 ounces Brie cheese, cut into 8 (1-inch) circles
8 walnut halves
salt and freshly ground pepper to taste

For the hoagie, preheat the broiler to 300 degrees. Cut off the ends of the miniature loaves and split them horizontally along the long side, cutting to but not through the opposite side. Spread 1/4 of the goat cheese on the bottom half of each loaf.

Place the loaves on a broiler pan and broil for 2 to 3 minutes or until the cheese is melted and golden brown. Add the lettuce and tomato and cut the loaves into halves to serve.

For the grilled cheese, place each slice of cheese between 2 slices of bread and sprinkle it with salt and pepper.

Melt the butter in a large sauté pan and sauté the sandwiches in the butter until golden brown. Trim the crusts and cut each sandwich into 2 rectangles to serve.

For the mini Brie sandwiches, preheat the broiler to 300 degrees. Trim the crusts from the bread and cut each slice into two 2-inch squares. Cut a hole in the center of 8 squares with a 1-inch cutter.

Stack the squares with holes on the squares without holes. Place 1 piece of cheese into each hole and top with a walnut half; sprinkle with salt and pepper.

Place on a broiler pan and broil for 3 1/2 minutes or until the cheese melts.

TIP: You can stick a clean new golf tee through each sandwich for the full effect!

TOMATO SOUP

RATING: A Short Par 3; Average Greens Fees

SERVES: 4

If tomatoes are in season and exuding late-summer flavor, then you have perfect conditions to make tomato soup. The sweet roasted garlic and fresh herb garnishes add interest and complement the silky smooth soup. Don't sweat it with this dish; a chiffonade is simply a fancy term for confetti-like strips.

> 2 tablespoons olive oil
> 1/2 cup finely chopped onion
> 1 garlic clove
> chiffonade of 6 fresh basil leaves
> 6 sprigs fresh thyme
> 4 cups coarsely chopped seeded Roma tomatoes
> 4 cups water
> 1/2 cup tomato paste
> 1 tablespoon sugar
> 1 1/2 teaspoons salt
> Oven-Roasted Garlic, for garnish (page 40)
> chiffonade of 3 basil leaves, for garnish

Heat the olive oil in a large saucepan and add the onion, garlic, chiffonade of 6 basil leaves and the thyme. Sweat over low heat until the onion is translucent. Add the tomatoes and water and simmer for 30 minutes.

Process the soup in batches in a blender until smooth, filling the blender only halfway each time; the soup is very hot, and it is important to fill the blender only halfway to avoid splashing and serious injury.

Strain the batches back into the saucepan. Whisk in the tomato paste, sugar and salt. Simmer for 15 minutes. Ladle into soup bowls and garnish with Oven-Roasted Garlic and basil chiffonade. Serve immediately.

TIP: To make a chiffonade, stack the leaves and roll them into a tight tube, then slice across the tube to create thin strips.

OVEN-ROASTED GARLIC

RATING: A Short Par 3; Low Greens Fees

SERVES: A Crowd

Gilroy, California, which bills itself as the garlic capital of the world, is located just a hop, skip, and a jump from the Monterey Peninsula. At the Annual Garlic Festival there, people can sample garlic dishes ranging from the savory to the sweet. (Think garlic ice cream!) I, too, share their sentiment about celebrating garlic's amazing versatility. In this preparation, garlic's natural sugars caramelize to produce a soft and mellow flavor.

4 whole garlic heads
1 tablespoon salt
1/4 teaspoon freshly ground pepper (optional)
1/4 cup sugar
2 cups olive oil or canola oil

Preheat the oven to 300 degrees. Cut off the tops of the garlic heads, leaving the heads intact. Place them cut side up in a small 2-inch-deep baking pan.

Season the garlic evenly with the salt, pepper and sugar; add enough olive oil to cover the heads completely. Cover the baking pan with foil and roast for 30 minutes.

TIP: Serve with a good crusty bread for dipping into the garlic-infused oil. The roasted garlic can also be removed from the peel and smeared on bread, served as a garnish, or tossed with pasta, rice, or mashed potatoes.

CAESAR SALAD WITH CRUNCHY SARDINES

RATING: A Short Par 4; Average Greens Fees

SERVES: 2 to 4

Crisp sardines from the waters off Monterey replace the Caesar salad's classic use of anchovies and croutons. Though this is a signature dish of southern California, I'm confident that even the Hollywood set who frequently visit Pebble Beach will approve of my locally inspired spin on the famous salad!

Caesar Dressing
2 egg yolks*
1 garlic clove
1 tablespoon drained capers
1/2 cup (2 ounces) grated Parmesan cheese
2 teaspoons Dijon mustard
5 teaspoons freshly squeezed lemon juice
1/2 cup water
1/4 teaspoon salt
1/2 teaspoon freshly ground pepper
1 1/4 cups olive oil

Salad
1 large head romaine, coarsely chopped
1 can sardines packed in oil
2 tablespoons butter, softened
1/4 cup panko (Japanese bread crumbs)
freshly ground pepper to taste

For the dressing, process the egg yolks, garlic, capers, Parmesan cheese and Dijon mustard in a blender. Add the lemon juice, water, salt and pepper and blend.

Drizzle in the olive oil gradually, processing constantly until the dressing is emulsified. Check and adjust the seasoning.

For the salad, preheat the broiler. Combine the dressing with the lettuce in a bowl and toss to coat evenly.

Arrange the sardines on a small baking sheet. Coat each sardine with the softened butter and bread crumbs; season lightly with pepper. Broil for 1 to 2 minutes or until golden brown. Place the crisp sardines on the salad and serve immediately.

*To avoid the danger of salmonella in uncooked egg yolks, you can use an equivalent amount of pasteurized egg substitute.

Bistro-Style Braised Lamb Shanks

RATING: Par for the Course on a Par 4; Average Greens Fees

SERVES: 4

After a lot of golf, I crave hearty comfort food like a lamb stew. This fortifying dish is especially fitting after a round played under the foggy and chilly conditions of the Monterey Peninsula and its extreme "Crosby Weather." The glossy sauce that coats the braised meat is also delicious over fluffy mashed potatoes.

4 (8- to 10-ounce) lamb shanks
1 tablespoon salt
2 cups chopped onions
1 cup chopped peeled carrots
1 cup chopped celery
4 large garlic cloves, mashed
4 sprigs fresh thyme
1 bay leaf
1 (6-ounce) can tomato paste
6 cups (about) water
1 tablespoon chopped fresh
    parsley, for garnish

Preheat the oven to 400 degrees. Place the lamb shanks in a medium ovenproof stockpot and season with the salt.

Sprinkle the onions, carrots, celery, garlic, thyme and bay leaf evenly over the lamb. Blend the tomato paste with enough water to cover the shanks in a bowl and pour over the lamb.

Roast for about 1¹/2 hours or until the meat pulls away from the bone. Strain the cooking liquid from the lamb and vegetables and return it to the stockpot. Cook the liquid until reduced by ¹/4.

Remove the lamb to a serving plate. Discard the bay leaf and spoon the reduced cooking liquid over the top; sprinkle with the parsley to serve.

TIP: As with any stew, it is best to prepare this dish ahead of time so that the flavors become more complex.

A GOLFING PILGRIMAGE **PEBBLE BEACH**

BUTTERY WHIPPED POTATOES

RATING: Par for the Course on a Par 4; Low Greens Fees

SERVES: 4 to 6

For the ultimate mashed potatoes, you must pull out all of the stops and use rich products like heavy cream and butter. The secret to making creamy whipped potatoes and avoiding a gluey mess is to make sure that all of the ingredients remain HOT while mixing.

6 potatoes
2 tablespoons salt
8 cups (about) water
2 cups heavy cream
1 cup (2 sticks) butter
salt and freshly ground pepper to taste

Peel the potatoes and cut them into large pieces. Combine with 2 tablespoons salt and enough water to cover in a saucepan. Cook for 20 to 25 minutes or until tender; drain. Place the potatoes in a bowl of a mixer fitted with a whip attachment and whisk at low speed.

Combine the cream and butter in the same saucepan used to cook the potatoes. Bring just to a boil.

Add the cream mixture to the potatoes gradually, whisking constantly at low speed. Increase the speed as the cream begins to be incorporated and whip until smooth. Season with salt and pepper to taste.

BRAISED ARTICHOKE HEARTS WITH CORIANDER AND WHITE WINE

RATING: Par for the Course on a Par 5, Average Greens Fees

SERVES: 4

Artichokes may be the signature dish for the Monterey Peninsula, for these beauties are found growing in abundance in the nearby town of Castroville, California, and chances are that the fresh artichokes that you buy at your local grocery come from this very place. To choose the best artichoke, look for one with evidence of a little brown kiss of frost on the tips of its outer leaves; it will yield a sweet heart. Reserve the artichokes in a bowl of lemon water to keep them from turning black before cooking.

> *3 tablespoons olive oil*
> *1 medium carrot, sliced*
> *2 ribs celery, sliced*
> *1/2 onion, sliced*
> *2 garlic cloves*
> *1 teaspoon coriander seeds*
> *1 sprig thyme*
> *1/2 teaspoon black peppercorns*
> *1 bay leaf*
> *4 artichoke hearts, leaves and stems removed*
> *1 cup white wine*
> *2 cups Vegetable Stock (page 181)*
> *salt and freshly ground pepper to taste*

Heat the olive oil in a large shallow saucepan over low heat. Add the carrot, celery, onion, garlic, coriander seeds, thyme, peppercorns and bay leaf. Sweat until the vegetables' juices are released without browning.

Add the artichoke hearts and continue to sweat. Increase the heat to medium-high and add the white wine. Cook until the liquid is reduced by 1/2. Add the Vegetable Stock and season with salt and pepper. Cover with a circle of parchment and cook for 20 minutes or until tender.

Cool to room temperature and store in the refrigerator in the braising liquid until needed. Discard the bay leaf before serving. Serve warm or cold. You can stuff them with an herbed goat cheese and broil just before serving, or simply slice and serve as the side dish to complement a hearty main dish.

TIP: Your equipment is key to the success of this dish. Before beginning to trim the artichokes, make sure that you are working with a well-sharpened paring knife. Most accidents with a knife occur when the blade is dull and the user is forcing the knife rather than letting the blade do the work. Try using a grapefruit spoon with a serrated tip to dig out the thistles in the inner choke.

PINE NUT TART

RATING: A Long Par 4; High Greens Fees

SERVES: 8

This tart is a perfect dish for so many times of the day or evening. I think this dish, chock full of delicious pine nuts, is meant to be enjoyed over a leisurely brunch just as well as in the afternoon with a glass of wine or for dessert after a meal. Whichever way, it always gives me a serene feeling and I think of driving on Pebble Beach's seventeen-mile drive amid the cypress trees and Monterey pines.

1 recipe Pâte Sucrée (page 187), chilled
1 cup (2 sticks) butter, softened
2¹/4 cups confectioners' sugar
3 eggs
1¹/2 cups almond powder
¹/4 cup flour
2 tablespoons dark rum
1¹/2 cups Pastry Cream (page 184)
1¹/3 cups pine nuts

Preheat the oven to 350 degrees. Line a 10-inch tart pan with the chilled Pâte Sucrée. Prick the dough with a fork to help release steam. Bake for about 15 minutes or until the edges are light brown and the center is slightly dry. Cool to room temperature. Maintain the oven temperature.

Cream the butter and confectioners' sugar in a bowl of a mixer fitted with a paddle attachment until light and fluffy. Add the eggs, almond powder and flour gradually in the order listed, mixing until smooth. Fold in the rum and Pastry Cream.

Spoon into the tart shell and sprinkle the top with the pine nuts. Bake for about 25 minutes or until the filling is set and the pine nuts give off their sweet and nutty aroma. Cool on a wire rack.

TIP: You can line the tart shell with foil or baking parchment and fill with pie weights or dried beans to bake; it will keep it from blistering or rising.

All the holes at the Ojai
Country Club Golf
Course offer stunning
panoramic views of the
Topa Topa Mountains.

RUSTIC SHANGRI-LA

OJAI

California

I rolled into Ojai after a 45-minute

scenic country drive on the back roads

from Santa Barbara. Soaking in the magnificent

springtime scenery on California Highway 150, the

scent of orange blossoms in the air beckoning

from the area's surrounding groves, and the warm

sun that radiated a feeling of overall well-being,

I entered what some have dubbed The New Age

capital. As I pulled into my destination, the Ojai Valley

Inn & Spa, I was struck by the dramatic panoramic

beauty of the Topa Topa Mountains, which overlook

the valley and the resort's famous golf course.

It was easy to settle into the gracious Spanish colonial-style lodging, and I was soon treated to a spectacular front row view of "The Pink Moment"— a local's phrase that aptly describes the special phenomenon which occurs at dusk, when the sun reflects off the nearby Pacific Ocean and creates a pink hue on the mountains. The soothing atmosphere of soft pink light provided the perfect metaphor for what proved to be a paradisaic experience over the next few days.

I started my first full day with a round of golf at the Ojai Country Club Golf Course. Through the years, this 6,156-yard par 70 has been the site of seven Senior PGA tournaments. What I find so special about this course are the amazing panoramic views of the mountains from every hole. Two holes, in particular, the course's so-called "Lost Holes," which are holes 7 and 8, both provide the perfect blend of challenge, beauty, and even historic intrigue. These holes were originally holes 3 and 4 when George C. Thomas, Jr.'s, course first opened in 1923. The course's integrity of design became compromised, however, during World War II, when the United States Army and Navy took over the resort as a training camp and then an "R & R" facility. When the government restored and rebuilt the course before returning the property to private ownership, it did not follow Thomas' design and these two holes were lost. I am sure glad that they have since been found! It was not until 1999, after careful research into Thomas' architectural plans, that these two original holes were restored.

Hole 7 at Ojai, designed by Thomas as a tribute to his favorite hole, number 3 at Pine Valley, is a 203-yard par 3 with seven bunkers that front the green. Ball placement is key, as the green is bordered on the left by a steep, 50-foot gully and out-of-bounds play on the right. When Ben Crenshaw played it, he said that it required the perfect shot. I took Crenshaw's word and visualized hitting that ball square to place it on the green. The positive thoughts paid off, and I putted in for a birdie. The excitement on the 7th carried me for the rest of the day!

Hole 8, the other "Lost Hole," is especially tricky because the small-face bunker, which is set back about ten yards from the front of the green, creates the illusion that the shot is shorter than it actually is. I was forewarned and played the hole conservatively, for a bogey.

Between picking up pointers from the golf pro, I discovered a variety of wild herbs growing along the fairways. Fragrant fennel, poppies, rosemary, and thyme provided the trip's first culinary inspiration. I set up a grill in the inn's vast, cultivated organic herb garden to prepare a quick and delicious lunch of local foods. I supplemented the fairway herbs with a mixed bouquet from the inn's herb garden and made a compound herb butter to slather on fresh spotted prawns, which I grilled and plated over some micro greens with orange- and maple syrup-glazed carrots en papillote. In a matter of a few minutes, I prepared a feast from fresh, local ingredients; virtually nothing came from more than ten miles away.

The outstanding Santa Barbara County Gainey chardonnay that I ordered to accompany lunch spurred me on to become better acquainted with the local wine industry. The visitor center at the Ojai Valley Chamber of Commerce is a valuable source of information, not only for the locations of more than 40 local wineries but also for pointing out the location of Bart's Books.

Browse over 100,000
used books on the shelves
at Bart's Books in Ojai.

This unusual bookstore is located just a block north of the visitor's center. Here the bookworm in me found the ultimate bookstore Shangri-La of over 100,000 used books set up under tree-shaded patios. There is something sublime about browsing books alfresco amid lavender-scented breezes and a tree canopy, not to mention the relaxing effects of this veritable temple to literary pursuits.

I returned to the grounds of the resort, at once understanding Frank Capra's choice to film the 1937 classic *Lost Horizon* here. As a chef, I appreciate the area's richness on many levels, not the least of which are the dining possibilities. The menus of the inn's casual Oak Café and fine dining restaurant, Maravilla, are filled with the fabulous Central Coast cuisine. The inn's extensive three-acre hillside herb garden produces edible flowers and an abundance of fresh lettuces. Tomatoes, citrus, and other fruits and vegetables harvested nearby are typically served at the resort later that day. Local farmers, fishmongers, cheese makers, and ranchers supply additional menu ingredients year-round from the blend of ocean, mountain, and tropical microclimates for which Ojai has become famous. Don't miss the opportunity to sip the resort's aptly named signature cocktail, "The Pink Moment," from the Oak Café's outdoor terrace. Here, surrounded by ancient oak trees, savor and enjoy the evening's eponymous spectacle as a final symphonic course for the senses.

The following day, my planned afternoon trek to a few wineries turned into a mission to find the perfect pairing for the treasure I found during the morning's golf game. The giant porcini mushroom that I discovered at the base of an oak tree on the 11th hole was the icing on the cake, so to speak, for a most memorable round. So I packed a light picnic, and with prized mushroom in hand, set out for a motorcycle adventure to a few local wineries.

I found the staff at Gainey Vineyards in Santa Ynez to be particularly amicable and knowledgeable. Dan Gainey was a gracious host. He welcomed me into his cellaring room, where we barrel-tasted new vintages. His pinot noir is a true king in the making. I was already a fan of Gainey's chardonnay, whose crispness and subtle hints of oak have always stood out for me as one of the top American chardonnay wines. As we sampled his varietals, Dan gave me some background about his family's operation. The largest diversified ranchers in the Santa Ynez Valley, the Gainey Ranch businesses include cattle farming and Arabian horse breeding, as well as their vineyards. Their approach to farming has carried over to their approach to making fine wines. The two distinctly different microclimates that exist in the valley lend themselves to totally different wine varietals. Gainey's northern boundary is planted in the bordeaux varietals: sauvignon blanc, merlot, and cabernet franc, while their property on the western end of the valley, a cooler growing region more suitable for burgundian varietals, grows chardonnay, pinot noir and syrah grapes.

I knew Dan was someone who understood *terroir*, the soul of the soil, and would also take pleasure in finding a well-suited match to my porcini. I was happy to cook if he wouldn't mind supplying the kitchen. We agreed to pool our talents and resources on our search to discover the best pairing of wine and mushroom. The Gainey merlot did have its merits; however, we decided that the earthy and full-bodied pinot noir was a better complement to my mushroom bruschetta. As I sat at a picnic table in the vineyard's garden with my new friend, savoring a simple, but perfect, culinary marriage, I surveyed the splendor of the vineyards and noted another perfect marriage, that of nature and art. I felt we had truly dined on a slice of joie de vivre.

In an area so rich in natural resources, it was inspiring to see how much the local producers and naturalist refuges reach out to the public. I found it difficult to choose where to spend the remainder of my time. The Krotona Institute of Theosophy's grounds offer spectacular views from a 115-acre wooded estate with lily ponds and architecture in the Spanish colonial style. It is open to the public daily. This was definitely a

as evidenced by the easy and open way in which the staff of Gainey Winery greeted me and ventured with me on a culinary quest. And it is apparent in the way local entities remain devoted to preserving the environment by fostering active relationships with the public.

Even the spa staff's voices work their magic to quiet and relax the spirit with their soothing tones. The Ojai Valley Inn & Spa understands the relationship between peaceful mind, body, and soul and clearly had the principle of *terroir* at the heart of its treatments. The rose petal massage and lavender aromatherapy treatments derive their main ingredients from the inn's hillside herb garden. These ingredients are fully used to

The Ojai Valley Inn & Spa understands the relationship between peaceful mind, body, and soul.

possibility for a prime picnicking destination. I also considered the International Center for Earth Concerns for its guided bird walks in its South African, Australian, and native Californian botanic gardens and oak groves. I chose an early morning at Lake Casitas Recreation Area, just five miles southwest, to try my hand at trout fishing. Having just enjoyed the fruits of the Pacific Ocean the day before, I was lured by the lake's offerings and its stunning natural setting. I rounded out the day's dining experience and communion with nature at the Ranch House in Ojai. The temperate weather allows for dining in the Japanese garden, where you are treated to a stellar meal and soothed by gentle burbles from the nearby meandering streams.

By this time, I had begun to settle into the rhythm of Ojai's gentle, good life. It is present in natural states, such as the blending of water, light, and land that results in the "Pink Moment." It is woven into the social fabric,

nourish all our senses: evoking the tantalizing views of color and texture found in the garden itself; as an enhancement to the dining experience; and finally as a means to soothe the body and quiet the mind through our most primal sense, smell. The treatments brought my whole experience at Ojai full circle. I had immersed myself in the beauty of the land and the game of golf that I have come to love and which brought me here. By savoring these precious moments in life, I know that their effects will linger for a lifetime.

Departing Ojai, I couldn't help noticing the lingering fragrance of orange blossoms. Their languid perfume stayed on my mind, reminding me of a time well spent, while at the same time beckoning me to return to sample the mature pixie oranges in early fall. I looked forward to another opportunity to visit Ojai, where an autumn experience would surely have a personality all its own.

MUSHROOM BRUSCHETTA

RATING: Par for the Course on a Par 3; Average to High Greens Fees, depending on the type of mushroom

SERVES: 6 to 8

A rustic bite-size morsel whose earthy flavors scream "terroir," this first course is best started early in the day and left to rest so the flavor infuses into the bread. The topping can then be assembled quickly and cooked just before serving. If you are not using fresh porcini mushrooms, add some porcini powder, which can be purchased or made by grinding dried porcini mushrooms in a coffee mill or spice grinder.

1 baguette
2 whole garlic cloves
olive oil
salt and freshly ground pepper to taste
1 pound fresh mushrooms
2 garlic cloves, chopped
1/4 red onion, thinly sliced
1 teaspoon porcini powder
2 tablespoons chopped parsley
16 wide shavings Parmesan cheese

Preheat the broiler. Rub the bread crust with the whole cloves and slice as desired. Drizzle 1 side of each slice with olive oil and season with salt and pepper. Place on a baking sheet and toast lightly under the broiler; think medium-rare.

If using white mushrooms, include the stems and chop into small pieces. Heat a few tablespoons olive oil in a heated sauté pan. Add the mushrooms, chopped garlic and onion; sprinkle with salt, pepper and porcini powder. Sauté until heated through. Add the parsley and toss to mix well.

Spoon the mushroom mixture onto the bruschetta and top with Parmesan cheese shavings. Serve with a glass of pinot noir from Gainey Ranch, or hold your own tasting to decide for yourself the perfect culinary/wine pairing.

TIP: Rub the outside of the bread with garlic, especially if using a fresh loaf. The crust will act almost like sandpaper, whereas the inside of the bread is too soft to provide any resistance to the garlic.

RUSTIC SHANGRI-LA OJAI

Grilled Spotted Prawns with Herb Butter

RATING: A Short Par 3; High Greens Fees

SERVES: 4

This dish need not be limited to one season. If you've put your grill away for the winter months, try broiling large whole shrimp instead. Save any remaining herb butter for another use, such as a seasoning for roasting poultry. Though this dish calls for a veritable herbal bouquet, like I found in Ojai, other herb combinations can just as easily please your palate.

1/2 cup chopped fresh herbs, such as rosemary, parsley,
*   tarragon, chives, sage and fennel tops*
1 cup (2 sticks) butter, softened
1/4 cup finely ground bread crumbs
20 whole spotted prawns or shrimp in shells
salt and freshly ground pepper to taste

Mix the fresh herbs with the butter in a bowl. Add the bread crumbs and mix well.

Cut the unpeeled prawns into halves lengthwise, leaving the heads intact. Scrape out the veins and season with salt and pepper. Spread the butter mixture on the body portions.

Grill for several minutes or just until cooked through; the shell will be red and the butter melted. You can also place the prawns on a baking sheet and broil for 4 to 5 minutes.

Serve over mixed lettuce or micro greens seasoned with salt, pepper and a fruity olive oil.

OVEN-ROASTED CALIFORNIA SQUAB AU JUS

RATING: A Short Par 4; Average to High Greens Fees

SERVES: 4

The strength of this dish lies in its simple preparation, allowing the complexity of the flavors from the squab to resonate. This entrée, perfect in its simplest state, requires no embellishments, much like nearly every hole that I played on Ojai's golf course, which is perfectly situated with unobstructed mountain views.

4 squab, cleaned and dressed
4 tablespoons Garlic Butter (page 182)
salt and freshly ground pepper to taste
¹/₄ cup olive oil
2 garlic cloves
1 carrot, chopped
1 small onion, chopped
1 bay leaf
2 slices bacon, coarsely chopped
1 to 1¹/₂ cups water

Preheat the oven to 395 degrees. Rinse the squab and pat dry with a paper towel. Place 1 tablespoon of the Garlic Butter in the cavity of each squab and sprinkle with salt and pepper.

Heat the olive oil in a roasting pan on the stovetop and add the squab. Sear until golden brown on all sides. Add the garlic, carrot, onion and bay leaf. Cook for 2 minutes longer or until the vegetables are light brown. Sprinkle with the bacon.

Roast in the oven for 5 minutes on each side. Remove the squab to a warm plate. Place the roasting pan over medium-high heat on the stovetop and add the water.

Cook for 4 to 6 minutes, stirring occasionally with a wooden spoon to remove the browned bits from the bottom of the pan. Strain the cooking liquid and adjust the seasoning.

Remove the breasts and legs from each squab. Place on a serving plate and spoon the cooking liquid over the top.

CARROTS EN PAPILLOTE

RATING: A Short Par 3; Low Greens Fees

SERVES: 4

This is a versatile preparation for carrots. It can provide a different spin on a common vegetable side dish, or it can be one of the stars in a luncheon salad to accompany the Grilled Spotted Prawns on page 53.

3 large carrots or
    12 baby carrots
2 oranges
salt and freshly ground
    pepper to taste
1¹/2 tablespoons maple syrup

Peel the large carrots and slice lengthwise into quarters; leave baby carrots whole. Peel the oranges and slice ¹/2 inch thick, reserving any orange juice.

Arrange the orange slices on a large square of heavy-duty foil; arrange the carrots on the orange slices and season with salt and pepper. Drizzle with the maple syrup and any reserved orange juice. Seal the foil, leaving some space for the carrots to steam.

Grill the packet or bake in a hot oven for 15 to 20 minutes or until the carrots are tender-crisp.

TIP: After removing the cooked carrots, close the foil, leaving only a small opening. Drizzle the cooking juices from the opening over the carrots or use over a carrot and grilled prawn salad.

LAVENDER MADELEINES

RATING: Par for the Course on a Par 4; Average Greens Fees

MAKES: 6 dozen

Like golfing on a windy day, it is difficult to know how these capricious tiny cakes are going to behave. They are not necessarily hard to make; you just need to use a light touch when working with the batter. The madeleines' heady lavender aroma will quite possibly transport you to California's central coast, while their flavor is but a subtle hint of lavender on the palate.

1¹/2 cups (3 sticks) butter
¹/4 cup dried lavender blossoms
2 cups flour
2¹/2 teaspoons baking powder
¹/2 teaspoon salt
4 egg yolks
8 whole eggs
1¹/3 cups sugar

Combine the butter and lavender blossoms in a saucepan. Heat over low heat until the butter melts and is infused with the essence of the lavender. Strain, reserving the warm butter.

Sift the flour, baking powder and salt together. Combine the egg yolks, whole eggs and sugar in a mixing bowl and whisk until fluffy. Add the sifted dry ingredients and mix well. Add the warm butter in a steady stream, beating constantly at low speed.

Cover the mixture with plastic wrap and let stand in the refrigerator for 4 hours or longer.

Preheat the oven to 325 degrees. Spray madeleine molds with nonstick cooking spray or brush with clarified butter.

Spoon the batter into the prepared molds, filling ³/4 full. Bake for 5 to 7 minutes or until golden brown; do not overbake. Unmold the madeleines immediately; they tend to stick when cool. Serve with afternoon tea or as a refined last bite of a meal.

TIP: Ideally, madeleines should be served warm. If you must make them ahead of time, this is one of the rare times I recommend microwaving briefly before serving to soften and warm the delicate cakes.

PIXIE ORANGE TART

RATING: A Long Par 4; Average Greens Fees

SERVES: 6 to 8

Pixie oranges are smaller than the more readily available navel oranges. They are grown abundantly in Ojai, but they are hard to come by when I am cooking in Chicago. I find that the juicy seedless oranges that are available in my local markets work just fine, too.

12 pixie oranges or
   3 seedless oranges
1 cup sugar
1 vanilla bean, split lengthwise
3 to 4 cups water
Pâte Sucrée (page 187)
1/2 cup lemon curd (page 187)
8 ounces semisweet chocolate,
   melted (optional)

Rinse and dry the oranges. Cut them into 1/8-inch slices.

Sprinkle a thin layer of the sugar over the bottom of a 3-quart saucepan. Alternate layers of the orange slices and sugar in the prepared saucepan until all ingredients are used, ending with the sugar. Place the vanilla bean on top.

Add just enough water to cover the layers by pouring it gently down the side of the pan. Top with a circle of baking parchment. Cook over low heat for about 2 hours or until the orange slices are translucent, adding additional water if the cooking syrup becomes too thick. Cool to room temperature.

Preheat the oven to 325 degrees. Roll out the Pâte Sucrée and place it in a greased 9-inch tart pan. Prick the dough with a fork to release the steam while baking. Fill the shell with pie weights, rice or dried beans. Bake for 30 minutes; remove the weights. Maintain the oven temperature.

Drain the oranges, discarding the vanilla bean. Alternate layers of the oranges and lemon curd in the prepared tart shell until all ingredients are used. Bake for 18 to 20 minutes or until the tart shell is golden brown.

Cool the tart to room temperature. Cut into wedges and drizzle each serving with the melted chocolate.

TIP: A few minutes before the tart shell has finished baking, remove the weights and brush it with a wash made from cream, egg yolk and sea salt. This will protect the shell from becoming soggy.

I had never visited the desert Southwest, but when it came time to choose a destination for a golf getaway in this region, The Boulders Resort & Golden Door Spa in Carefree, Arizona, won my vote hands down. A recipient for the fifteenth consecutive year of the AAA 5-Diamond Award and home to two 18-hole Gold Medal golf courses, The Boulders offers world-class amenities, which are in harmony with its pristine, natural environment in a relaxed setting. The Boulders' 1,300 acres are an oasis of casual luxury within the expansive desert landscape.

While the desert is known for its intense heat in the summer months, its mild daytime climate in the latter part of winter, when I visited, gives way to chilly nights that are best spent near the radiant warmth of a fire. Arriving at The Boulders late in the evening, my initial impressions were formed by the spicy smoke coming from the shaggy bark juniper burning in the outdoor fireplace at the entry to the main lodge and by the buttery but substantial feel to the lodge's hand-rubbed wooden entry doors.

A second fireplace was ablaze inside the main lodge, creating an ambient and communal setting. From the main lodge, I got a quick lift on a golf cart to my casita, one of 160 individual adobe structures that make up the resort's guest accommodations. Each is outfitted with a wood-burning fireplace and plenty of shaggy bark juniper wood for creating the perfect atmosphere in a cozy desert retreat.

Ancient formations of granite tower above the 160 guest casitas of The Boulders Resort & Golden Door Spa.

THE VALLEY OF THE SUN
ARIZONA
Carefree

In the morning, I slid the wooden window shades to the side and came face-to-face with the textures and colors of the high Sonoran Desert. Directly ahead lay dusty tan-colored boulders that form what appears to be a precariously situated rock pile subject to movement at any given moment, but in fact are stable rock formations, which are 1.4 billion years old. Off in the distance, what is known as the Black Mountain range actually looked purple in the early morning sun. Wispy, feathery branches growing from muted green trunks of palo verde trees and lots of cacti contrasted with the deep green grass covering one of the nearby golf greens.

On foot this time, I retraced my route to the main lodge for breakfast in the Palo Verde Room. On my way, I saw and heard plenty of desert wildlife. I spotted quail, cotton-tailed bunnies, doves, cardinals, and some cactus wrens who were busy pecking away at the flesh on a majestic saguaro cactus. There were tell-tale signs that other animals had visited over the course of the night. Half-missing cactus pods on a prickly pear cactus had surely been some javelina's midnight snack. I breakfasted on a light buffet that featured an array of baked goods made on the premises: yogurt, granola, and an assortment of fresh and dried fruits.

There is so much to see and do at The Boulders, it is hard to decide what to do first. I was truly intrigued by the amazing rock formations visible all around, so I asked the concierge about them. I learned that a resident geologist, Richard Allen, gives geology walks through the boulders. The boulders themselves are composed of granite and date from the Precambrian Era; they are examples of some of the area's earliest rock formations. A walk with Richard across the street to Black Mountain is a good way to learn the difference between the older dark granite rock that once formed a continental mass and the invasive granite boulders that were once molten masses extruded from the earth's core. The darker granite has a good system of drainage and can support vegetation, like cacti. The reddish masses of boulders have weathered over time into their distinctive shapes by fracturing along parallel planes; they then became rounded and peeled in appearance by wind and rain.

An astronomer as well as a geologist, Richard loves rocks, whether they are on Earth or in space! Join him at night and get the rare opportunity to view and learn about the stars, planets in our solar system, and other galaxies. That's far out! Closer to home, so to speak, are many other outdoor activities in the area, like jeep tours, hikes, and helicopter tours. After considering all of the activities that are available to guests of the resort for exploring the

A RECIPIENT FOR THE FIFTEENTH CONSECUTIVE YEAR OF THE AAA 5-DIAMOND AWARD

area, I headed straight for the golf clubhouse! This is my idea of getting to know the area, its rocks, and its space.

I suggest planning for back-to-back days of golf in order to play both courses. Each day, The Boulders alternates its course designation for resort or club member play. On my first day, resort guests were playing the South Course. This par 71 covers 6,246 yards from the white tee. Designed by Jay Morrish, this is one of the earliest examples of a desert golf course. Many of its fairways, landscaped with indigenous desert scrub, require no external supply of water. The challenge to the uninitiated desert golfer, like myself, is not to become distracted by the unusual desert color and to keep the ball on the grass.

Teeing off at the 1st hole, a 381-yard par 4, was a tough start. I laid up on my shot and managed to keep my ball fair on the dogleg right with lateral hazards. I tried not to let the desert throw me off my game. I focused on playing conservatively, my simple strategy being to stay on the color green! The second shot was downhill into a narrow alley that bottlenecks right before the green. A giant boulder and the now-familiar signature rock pile set up right behind it. Another beauty that features close-ups of a rock pile is the 5th hole, a long par 5. I hit a 5-wood to the right side. From the middle of the fairway, I aimed for a lone saguaro cactus to help line up my approach shot.

Hole 7 features the most unusual rock formation that I encountered on my entire visit to The Boulders. The tremendous round boulder, known by locals as "Rosie's Rock," perches atop a rock base of

relatively modest proportions and seems to defy all notions of gravity. After close inspection of this remarkable boulder and the space that exists between this behemoth and its base, I turned my attention back to the hole. On this par 3, your first shot must carry over desert rough. I reached for a longer club to help contend with the large bi-level green. Throughout my round, the elevated tee boxes and desert landscape consistently called for careful club selection. The South Course was a lot of fun to play. I enjoyed the challenge that the desert created and the unusual rocky topography, as well as the course's dramatic elevation changes.

The North Course, by contrast, plays slightly longer but feels more manageable due to its wider and flatter valley fairways. The course, also a Jay Morrish design, has a nice rhythm and looks out to mountain views of Pinnacle Peak and Black Mountain. I spent the following day playing it and learning more about the two courses in general from valley native and Assistant Golf Pro Dean Ballard. I fished for any tips Dean might have for getting out of trouble in the desert and had the unfortunate luck a few times of having to apply his words of wisdom. Dean's advice to me was that if I managed to find my ball out there in the desert, I should play back to the fairway, not to the green. Laying up and playing smart is a must when playing each of The Boulders' 36 holes.

Holes 14 and 18 North provided surprise water obstacles in a course that otherwise features desert scrub that fronts and surrounds nearly every fairway. On 14, the 127-yard par 3 tees off over a pond. It was further complicated by a slight head wind. This was one of those rare instances while playing at The Boulders when I reached for more club. The 18th hole doglegs right. Because of a little lake hugging the left side of the fairway, I played the longer shot to avoid the water, then stayed right on my approach. Though desert surrounds the entire hole, there really is plenty of room to stay fair on this long par 4.

I think a lightbulb went off in Dean's head when I mentioned to him that I was a chef and was interested in learning more about the area's indigenous foods and local dining options. He described the "Tee Box Dinner" that The Boulders proudly offers to guests. Locations to choose from include a site with views of a lagoon and the clubhouse, a view looking out to the lights of Scottsdale, or a view of Rosie's Rock. Guests are treated to a candlelit sunset dinner highlighted by a formal table setting, music, and a three-course meal with wine, all brought to you by a personal server via a golf cart! The idea sounded tempting but better suited to later in the year when the evenings would be warmer.

Instead, I enjoyed a pleasant dinner indoors at Latilla, The Boulders' premier restaurant. Located in the main lodge, the relaxed but elegant setting glows under the signature latilla wood ceiling. Spanish for "little sticks," latillas filled in the spaces between large wooden beams in early pueblo dwellings of the Southwest. Picture windows line the curving walls of the restaurant and give glimpses of the adobe fireplace aglow just outside. Like its setting, the menu is not pretentious but, rather, offers fresh and delicious foods simply but skillfully prepared. The chef

begins each diner's meal by sending him or her a complimentary bite, or *amuse-bouche*. I appreciated the delectable morsel of half a boiled quail's egg and some caviar presented on a chilled silver spoon as I perused the ample wine list and menu. Northern California foie gras shares menu space with salmon mousse-filled cannelloni, New Zealand lamb, and Hawaiian mahimahi. The menu also features heart-healthy options, which reflect the spa cuisine found at The Golden Door. My delicious entrée of arctic char is proof that in this day and age, even a desert dweller can enjoy a fresh piece of fish from the other side of the globe.

After two consecutive days of golf, I looked forward to spending a day at the spa to complete the process of rejuvenation that a getaway to The Boulders delivers. The original Golden Door Spa in Escondido, California, is the oldest spa still in operation in the United States. When they opened at The Boulders in 2001, The Golden Door blended the natural environment and Native American heritage of the desert Southwest with the Japanese sensibility of its California location and concept. The result is a spacious adobe building that wraps almost seamlessly around the base of the famous rock pile. No right angles exist in the entire structure; rather, the smooth, rounded walls reflect a multicultural belief that positive energy flows continuously and should not be obstructed by sharp angles. I guess I buy into this, plus it looks pretty cool. At the center of the spa is the circular tearoom. More than a place for quiet meditation, it is also where people come for a morning energy boost.

Each day in the tearoom, the spa serves a warm tomato-base potassium broth to its guests. The tonic boosts blood sugar levels and replaces the body's vital balance of minerals. After an active morning spent working out, rock climbing, or playing golf, this is my idea of a reviving and delicious sports drink! It's no doubt that the Golden Door Spa places a lot of importance on fine cuisine. They have a large kitchen studio where healthy cooking demonstrations and lectures are given, and their heart-healthy spa cuisine sings with freshness and outstanding flavor. Enjoy a picturesque lunch or a smoothie on the spa's patio, which overlooks the rock pile and the pool complex.

While finishing my lunch there, I noticed a nearby teepee. Large enough to accommodate ten people, it is an authentic Navajo replica. A Native American shaman guides guests in meditation sessions and spiritual cleansing here through a smudging ceremony, using smoke and white sage from the grounds. I really wanted to indulge in a spa treatment that emphasized Native American traditions, so when I read about the various Arizona foods used in the turquoise wrap, The Golden Door's signature treatment, I knew I was hooked. This was the one I had to try.

Having now experienced the turquoise wrap, I know what it's like to be on the other side of the cooking process! Under warm, red lights, I steeped in a turquoise bath; I was scrubbed with Arizona blue cornmeal and I marinated while wrapped in a clay and ground turquoise mask as Janet, my therapist, surrounded me with the soothing sounds of a Native American rain stick and spicy aromatics. I was rinsed

under about eight Vichy showerheads before being glazed with warm Arizona honey. I finished the treatment with a visit to the steam room. Since my role with all of this food was not as chef, I decided to give in to the whole process and emerged feeling peaceful and content.

The Golden Door also has a sauna, an outdoor whirlpool with a cascading waterfall and meditation labyrinth, and an o'furo, a warm bath often found in Japanese Honjin inns. The choices for relaxation at the spa are endless. It's the perfect way to unwind after two great days of golf. Should you want to venture out beyond The Boulders, there are some nearby and not-so-nearby options.

Just a short walk away is El Pedregal, which is more than just a pleasant shopping complex. You can also enjoy the relaxing atmosphere and people-watching at its outdoor mall and fountain. Or walk through the Heard Museum North, an extension site of the notable Phoenix-based Heard Museum, to view exhibits on historic and contemporary Native Americans of the Southwest. There are several dining options at El Pedregal that complete The Boulders' restaurant repertoire. The Bakery Café has wonderful baked goods, as well as portable lunch fare perfectly suited for toting outdoors to enjoy as a picnic. Try a prickly pear margarita and Sonoran-style Mexican food at Cantina Del Pedregal, or if you're in the mood for something lighter, share some tapas-style dishes and choose from a wide array of cocktails at On the Rocks.

As a chef and owner of a bistro, I felt compelled to follow the buzz and met up with Matt Carter, one of this country's rising chefs. His Zinc Bistro, in the Kierland Commons just south on Scottsdale Road, has taken Scottsdale by storm with its sophisticated and innovative approach to dining. Here, a valley native has created a first-rate brasserie, serving up the caliber of food, service, and atmosphere one would come to expect in a large, cosmopolitan city. Matt personally types, prints, and develops the restaurant's ever-changing menus, so I knew he was the guy to ask about local and seasonal foods. Matt echoed Michael Hoobler, Executive Chef at The Boulders, with his wholehearted support and recommendation to check out one of their favorite suppliers, The Farm at South Mountain.

I could tell from Matt's comments regarding golf that he and Chef Hoobler might also share another thing in common besides their opinion of local food suppliers. Chef Hoobler had mentioned to me that although he enjoys the occasional round, he is liable to hit trees, carts, and other unintended objects. Matt, on the other hand, who plays in the valley's celebrity golf tournament sponsored by Bon Appétit every May, humbly accepts his role on the golf course, all in the name of charity, with his good-natured claim that somebody's got to lose! That "somebody" is typically Matt. Judging by their comments and having the distinct pleasure of trying their food, it is clear that one is safest with these chefs in the kitchen! I may not have picked up any golfing tips from Matt or Chef Hoobler, but their suggestion to visit Wayne Smith at The Farm did prove valuable.

I made the trek to The Farm, unprepared for what I would find, and I was truly blown away by the extent of its operation. I spotted owner and visionary Wayne Smith, tootling around the grounds on his golf cart.

Wayne took time to show me around, explaining how he helped to legislate an overlay district of mixed-use agriculture in this historically rural area, which is fast becoming industrialized. Wayne likes to refer to the zone as a "lifestyle district," where he aims to teach people a gentler lifestyle. Wayne's property sits on a 12-acre pecan-tree grove, which forms a sort of midway for picnickers. During the winter harvest, he encourages people to come collect pecans and reconnect to the land and the seasons. The nearby Farm Kitchen, located on the premises in a 1927 farmhouse with a charming brick patio, makes a mean pecan pie for those who miss the opportunity to harvest.

At the far end of the property, we came upon another little farmhouse, called Cottage Grove Antiques, which sits in front of The Farm's citrus and stone-fruit groves. Garden Territory, yet another retail store on the grounds, sells potted herbs, plants, and flowers, as well as books and other food- and gardening-related gifts. I discovered some amazing Arizona honeys here. Garden Territory also acts as a local outreach to the community through school programs and by offering mini-classes to the public. Resident experts and guest lecturers regularly give instruction in cooking, painting, and horticulture. Its pleasant, semi-enclosed setting makes it very homey.

I think homey is the best way to describe The Farm at South Mountain. Wayne has created a welcome feeling for all who come and encourages his visitors to stay and enjoy all of the resources. His motto is, "If you're in a hurry, come back another time." Luckily I had the time to continue to explore. We walked through the working organic farm. Edible flowers grew near rows of sugar snap peas and fava beans.

Lettuces in countless varieties grew amid chard and multi-colored beets. Carrots, fennel, and a host of herbs also grew in abundance. Wayne, an accomplished landscape architect with a small-town sensibility, is an informed, environmentally friendly farmer. He rotates and staggers his crops and treats them only with horticultural soap. The Farm's Saturday farmer's market attracts valley locals who want a glimpse of this bucolic existence while shopping for superb organic produce.

Our final stop on the grounds was at Quiessence, The Farm's gourmet restaurant, serving lunch six days a week and dinner on Thursdays and Fridays. We sat in the glass-enclosed patio of the original ranch-style farmhouse and enjoyed delicacies from farm to table. Before we even ordered, a dish of house-cured olives and little condiments of onion marmalade, eggplant, and tomato caviar were placed on our table. The gracious service may be a mainstay here, but the inspired menu changes monthly with the seasons. We started with a salad of freshly picked mesclun and three types of beets from The Farm. Shaved fennel and a blood orange vinaigrette, both products of The Farm, accentuated perfectly seared sea scallops. Breads are all made here. The mushroom pizza, made in the outdoor adobe oven, was outstanding. For dessert, we enjoyed the pecan honey ice cream and the almond shortbread that came garnished with berries, crème fraîche, basil syrup, and aged balsamic vinegar. The Farm at South Mountain is a very special place. My experience here with Wayne allowed me the chance to get to know the special attributes of the desert Southwest, especially in a culinary sense.

My first visit to this vast desert and mountainous region produced not one but two oases. The Farm is truly a pleasure for the senses and a place to enjoy all the creative impulses of those who make this their home away from home. The Boulders in Carefree is another haven. You will love every minute of your

Rosie's Rock, on the 7th hole of The Boulders' South Course

time spent here. Catch some downtime at The Golden Door Spa, sample from the various dining options at The Boulders, swing away on the 36 holes of championship desert golf, and relax in the casually elegant lodgings that blend so well into the desert landscape and breathtaking beauty of the boulders. Seek out these special desert destinations and take the time to immerse yourself in all that they offer.

CACTUS PEAR MARTINI

RATING: Par for the Course on a Par 3; Average to High Greens Fees

MAKES. 1 drink

Start the evening with a glass of this beautiful liquid-magenta Arizona sunset, livened with a touch of citrus. Ripe prickly pears are summertime fruits, purplish-red in color, that are available fresh in specialty stores. Be sure to strain the seeds from the pulp. Sometimes straight prickly pear juice is also available.

1 1/2 ounces (3 tablespoons) Tequila Anejo
1/2 ounce (1 tablespoon) Cointreau
1 ounce (2 tablespoons) orange juice
1/4 ounce (1/2 tablespoon) lime juice
splash of lemon-lime soda
1 ounce (2 tablespoons) prickly pear purée
1/4 ounce (1/2 tablespoon) sweet-and-sour mix
ice
1 orange slice, for garnish
1 lime peel twist, for garnish
1 maraschino cherry

Combine the Tequila, Cointreau, orange juice, lime juice and lemon-lime soda in a cocktail shaker. Add the prickly pear purée, sweet-and-sour mix and ice and shake to chill well. Strain into a martini glass. Garnish with an orange slice, lime peel twist and maraschino cherry.

Braised Rabbit Terrine with Sage

RATING: A Long Par 5; Average to High Greens Fees

SERVES: 8

Rabbit is often overlooked in the United States, yet its lean meat is a natural for people who are watching their fat intake but still like a lot of flavor. The lengthy braising time, essential for tenderizing the meat, and the multi-step recipe may seem daunting, but it's well worth the effort. So dig in your heels and try this tasty and somewhat unusual dish. The terrine is a great starter for dinner parties or can be cut into bite-size pieces as an hors d'oeuvre.

olive oil
2 rabbits, each cut into 6 pieces
salt and freshly ground pepper to taste
2 medium carrots, cut into large pieces
2 ribs celery, cut into large pieces
1 medium onion, cut into large pieces
1 garlic head, sliced into halves crosswise
2 bay leaves
2 teaspoons chopped sage
1 bouquet garni of 1 bay leaf, parsley and fresh
    thyme sprigs tied around a celery rib

1 teaspoon herbes de Provence
1 teaspoon tomato paste
4 cups white wine
8 cups Chicken Stock (page 179)
2 tablespoons finely chopped carrot
1 1/2 tablespoons chopped parsley
1 1/2 tablespoons chopped sage
3 tablespoons chopped seeded peeled tomato
7 gelatin leaves, softened in cold water, or
    1 ounce powdered gelatin

Heat several tablespoons of olive oil in a large stockpot. Season the rabbit with salt and pepper and sear in batches in the heated oil until golden brown on all sides, adding additional olive oil to the stockpot as needed. Remove the rabbit to a platter and reserve.

Add 2 carrots, the celery, onion and garlic to the stockpot and cook until caramelized. Stir in the bay leaves, 2 teaspoons chopped sage, the bouquet garni, herbes de Provence and tomato paste. Return the rabbit pieces and accumulated juices to the stockpot. Add the white wine and scrape the browned bits from the bottom of the stockpot. Cook until reduced by 1/2.

Add the Chicken Stock and braise for several hours or until the rabbit meat is tender enough to fall from the bones. Remove the rabbit to a covered container, reserving the cooking liquid. Chill the rabbit in the refrigerator. Strain the reserved cooking liquid and return to the stockpot. Cook over medium-high heat until reduced by 1/2. Add the softened gelatin leaves and stir to dissolve completely.

Debone the cooled rabbit, discarding the skin and bones. Combine with 2 tablespoons carrot, the parsley, 1 1/2 tablespoons chopped sage and the tomato in a bowl and mix gently. Spread a layer of the rabbit mixture in a terrine and add enough of the braising liquid to cover the mixture; press the liquid with a fork to make an even layer. Repeat the process until the terrine is full. Do not add all of the meat mixture and liquid at once, or the meat will settle to the bottom, making an uneven terrine.

Chill in the refrigerator for 1 to 1 1/2 hours or until firm. Slice and serve with a light vinaigrette, mixed greens and toast points.

TIP: Wait a day before reducing the strained braising liquid and building the terrine. This will help break up the work as well as allow the flavors to intensify and blend.

Oven-Roasted Marinated Quail with Red and Yellow Tomato Salad

SERVES: 4

When tomatoes are at their peak of flavor, they make a colorful and tasty backdrop to tender roasted quail. Outside the Valley of the Sun, you might not find this bird at your local grocery store. Try a purveyor of game or a specialty market.

Marinated Quail	**Red and Yellow Tomato Salad**
juice of 1 orange	*2 red tomatoes*
juice of 1 lemon	*2 yellow tomatoes*
1 teaspoon whole grain mustard	*2 tablespoons olive oil*
1 cup olive oil	*salt and freshly ground pepper to taste*
1 teaspoon thyme	*1 tablespoon herbes de Provence*
1 bay leaf	*1/2 cup Balsamic Vinaigrette (page 176)*
4 quail	

For the marinated quail, combine the orange juice, lemon juice, whole grain mustard, olive oil, thyme and bay leaf in a large bowl and mix well. Cut each quail into halves and add to the marinade. Marinate for about 1 hour.

Preheat the oven to 375 degrees. Remove the quail from the marinade and place in a roasting pan; discard the bay leaf. Insert a meat thermometer into the thickest portion of 1 quail half; do not allow the thermometer to touch the bone. Roast to 160 degrees on the meat thermometer.

For the salad, slice the tomatoes 1/2 inch thick. Drizzle a baking pan with olive oil and arrange the tomato slices in a single layer in the pan. Season with salt, pepper and herbes de Provence. Roast just until warm but not soft.

To serve, place 1 slice of red tomato and 1 slice of yellow tomato on each plate. Top with 2 halves of roasted quail and drizzle with Balsamic Vinaigrette.

TIP: You may also prepare the oven-cured tomatoes the night before, following the directions above and placing the tomatoes in a 350-degree oven. Turn off the oven immediately and leave the tomatoes in the oven to cure overnight, concentrating their sugars.

SNOW PEAS WITH DATES

RATING: A Short Par 3; Average Greens Fees

SERVES: 4

The Farm at South Mountain grows some of the sweetest snow peas that I've tried. I couldn't resist Wayne's kind invitation to help myself to a few—and a few more! If you manage to get some of these sweeties home, this is an easy preparation that shows off the intense bright color and snap of the vegetables. By contrast, the almost candied sweetness of the dates, another Arizona treasure, and the mellow toasted almonds add dimensions of flavor and texture.

¹/₄ cup sliced almonds
salt to taste
1 pound snow peas, ends and fibrous edges removed
1 tablespoon butter
8 large dates, pitted and cut into thin strips
freshly ground pepper to taste

Preheat the oven to 225 degrees. Spread the sliced almonds on a baking sheet. Toast until light golden brown and fragrant.

Bring salted water to a boil in a saucepan. Add the snow peas and blanch; shock in an ice water bath to stop the cooking and drain; the snow peas should brighten in color but remain crisp.

Melt the butter in a sauté pan. Add the dates and sauté until almost candied. Add the almonds and then the snow peas; toss to coat well. Season with salt and pepper.

COWBOY BEANS

RATING: A Long Par 3; Low Greens Fees

SERVES: 4 to 6

When the nights get a little chilly, this hearty bean dish hits the spot. It's a great accompaniment to a steak dinner, or can be a meal in itself. This is a perfect do-ahead dish. Like so many other comfort foods, it reheats very well and might even taste better the next day.

> 1³/4 cups dried navy beans
> ¹/4 cup olive oil
> 2 tablespoons butter
> 1 medium onion, chopped
> 2 plum tomatoes, coarsely chopped
> salt and freshly ground pepper to taste
> 1 smoked ham hock
> 1 bouquet garni of part of a leek, 1 leafy celery rib,
>   ¹/2 of a carrot, fresh parsley, thyme sprigs and rosemary,
>   tied with kitchen twine
> 1 garlic head with the top sliced off
> 4¹/2 cups Vegetable Stock (page 181)
> 2 tablespoons butter

Combine the dried beans with enough water to cover well in a large saucepan. Soak for 8 hours or longer; drain.

Heat a large saucepot and add the olive oil and 2 tablespoons butter. Add the onion and tomatoes and season with salt and pepper. Cover tightly and sweat over low heat for a few minutes. Add the ham hock and continue to sweat. Add the bouquet garni, garlic head and drained beans. Continue to sweat for a few minutes.

Stir in the Vegetable Stock and place a round piece of parchment the size of the stockpot directly on top of the beans. Increase the heat and simmer for about 1 hour and 20 minutes or until the beans are tender. Remove the parchment, bouquet garni and garlic head. Stir in 2 tablespoons butter and adjust the seasoning.

TIP: If you would like a vegetarian version of this recipe, substitute 1 teaspoon coriander seeds for the ham hock.

Grilled Steak with Herb Butter

RATING: A Gimme; Average Greens Fees

SERVES: 4

The drive north on Scottsdale Road to The Boulders passes several historical, albeit commercial, cowboy steak places. This is my fail-proof recipe for a tasty and tender steak hot off the coals.

1 cup (2 sticks) butter, softened
1/2 cup chopped fresh herbs, such as tarragon, chives
    and parsley or rosemary and oregano
1/4 cup finely ground bread crumbs
2 pounds top round butt steak, sliced into
    4 (1-inch-thick) portions
salt and freshly ground pepper to taste

Cream the softened butter with the back of a wooden spoon in a mixing bowl. Add the herbs and then the bread crumbs, mixing well. Shape into a log and wrap in plastic wrap. Store in the refrigerator.

Preheat the grill. Season the steaks with salt and pepper. Grill on both sides to an internal temperature of 140 degrees or until done to taste.

Preheat the broiler. Place 2 ounces of the herb butter on the top of each steak and place on a broiler pan. Broil until the butter is golden brown. Serve immediately.

TIP: Purchase the steaks three or four days in advance. Remove the plastic wrap and allow the steaks to age in the refrigerator to tenderize.

HONEY ICE CREAM

RATING: A Long Par 4; Average Greens Fees

MAKES: 1 quart

Arizona honey comes in countless varieties and has many uses—besides its application for the turquoise wrap at The Golden Door Spa! I came across saguaro cactus flower honey and wild mountain pecan and mesquite honey, in addition to orange blossom and desert wildflower honeys at Garden Territory at The Farm at South Mountain. Choosing honey is similar to choosing wine and olive oil; taste a few kinds before making your final selection. Lavender honey is fragrant and medium-bodied, and I find that it works well for ice cream.

> *1 quart half-and-half*
> *10 egg yolks*
> *1/3 cup plus 1 tablespoon sugar*
> *1/2 cup honey*
> *1 drop of vanilla extract*

Bring the half-and-half to a simmer in a large saucepan. Whisk the egg yolks, sugar, honey and vanilla extract together in a bowl.

Stir half of the heated half-and-half into the egg yolks mixture to temper it; stir the egg yolks back into the half-and-half with a wooden spoon. Do not use a whisk at this point or you risk scrambling the egg yolks.

Heat over low heat to 172 degrees or until the mixture coats the back of a wooden spoon. Place the saucepan in an ice bath to chill the mixture.

Spoon into the container of an ice cream maker and churn until the ice cream forms soft peaks.

TIP: Serve the ice cream in orange cups for a beautiful presentation. To prepare, cut 1/4 inch off the tops of oranges and remove the fruit carefully, reserving the shells. You can freeze the shells immediately, or to remove some of their bitterness, you may blanche them in sweetened boiling water in a saucepan, shock in a ice bath and then freeze.

WORK
BECOMES
PLAY

KOHLER *Wisconsin*

The Blackwolf Run Course, designed by
Pete Dye, hugs the Sheboygan River,
where the salmon run spans from late
September to late October.

Too often in our daily lives we spend
countless hours of nearly every day hard at work.

We are either on the clock, so to speak, juggling the many activities that fill our familial duties, or moving at a frenetic pace getting to and from these various obligations. Seldom do we give ourselves permission to turn off the pressure cooker of life's responsibilities to focus on ourselves.

When I sense that a break from my daily duties as a chef is in order, Kohler really fits the bill. The American Club in Kohler, Wisconsin, is an easy 2½-hour drive from my hometown, Chicago, or an hour away from Milwaukee. Its world-class golf at Whistling Straits, Blackwolf Run, and unique Kohler Waters Spa has become a favorite getaway destination for me. This is a place where playfulness enters into the workplace and hard work can be made of play.

Though The American Club operates year-round, the golf courses do shut down for the winter months. The approximately seven-month season begins in April and ends with the second frost, occurring anywhere from the last week of October to mid-November. It was mid-October when I visited, and the Midwest was experiencing a mild autumn, an "Indian summer," so I figured that if I wanted one last chance to play the courses at Kohler this year, I had better seize the moment. Turning off the expressway to take the rural roads that lead to Kohler, I was treated to a beautiful display of fall splendor. The spent fields of corn contrasted with vibrant gold and crimson leaves, most of which remained on their branches but had begun to sprinkle the landscape in dappled, brilliant color.

Upon arrival, The American Club presents another dramatic visual effect with its formidable sprawling structure. The gabled brick exterior and slate tile roof evokes a sense of permanence with its rhythmic geometric forms. Indeed, the structure dates back to 1918 when Walter J. Kohler, the founder of Kohler Company, commissioned the building to house his company's immigrant workers. The waning need for worker housing eventually gave way to a new purpose for the main building.

Since 1981, The American Club has operated as a luxury hotel and has earned one of the only AAA 5-Diamond Ratings in the Midwest. To say that this company town has evolved over the years would be a huge understatement.

While still a family-run enterprise that remains true to its founding ideals, sport and leisure are now integral components of Kohler, and the quality of these offerings equals those attained by Kohler in the industrial arts. Though the workout complex, spa, and four world-class golf courses do dominate the resort atmosphere, Kohler's factory across the street continues to produce its signature state-of-the-art kitchen and bath fixtures and plumbing products. The building adjacent to the resort's spa is a great place to view all their products. Called the Kohler Design Center, it houses a three-story museum, an art gallery, and a design showroom.

Inside the American Club, the walls of its oak-paneled hallways proudly display photographs from its earlier days as well as portraiture featuring American leaders like Abraham Lincoln and George Washington. The lodge-like Lincoln Room, just off the main lobby, is a great sitting room in which to read the paper and enjoy morning and afternoon tea and coffee service. Each room in the main hotel is individualized to inspire its guests by commemorating an influential American and displaying a photograph of the individual, along with a brief biography or a piece of memorabilia once belonging to him or her. Signature Kohler products and fixtures are found in each room and throughout the resort as well. Perhaps the most telling evidence of the philosophy that shapes the resort's approach is the quote by Britain's John Ruskin that is emblazoned in the Wisconsin Room's leaded glass windows: "Life without labor is guilt—labor without art is brutality."

Ruskin's notion that work and art should go hand-in-hand is embodied even in the recent additions to the Kohler complex, where spa luxury elevates the common bathroom appliance and fixture to ethereal status. The new Kohler Waters Spa and Carriage House Inn is accessible to the main hotel by a subterranean walkway, a convenience during inclement weather but not always a necessity. Many of the Carriage House visitors focus strictly on the spa amenities. Donning the plush white robes and slippers provided by the resort, visitors here often opt to take all their meals on the premises and enjoy the freedom of pampered spa luxury. I planned to indulge in a few rejuvenating spa services, but first things first; I was here, after all, for the spectacular golf.

More than any other of The American Club's draws, the Whistling Straits, which are the Irish and the Straits courses, have put Kohler on the international map for must-visit golf destinations. Site of the 2004 PGA Championship, Pete Dye's Straits Course is the result of the total transformation of farmland into a sculpted but unmanicured and, therefore, untamed links course. Factor in the ocean-like expanse of mighty Lake Michigan as the backdrop to all 18 holes, rocky bluffs, sand dunes, and the strong prevailing winds with the 40-some Scottish blackface sheep that freely roam the Whistling Straits courses, and you might forget that you are golfing in the Midwest.

One of the course's most distinctive features is the natural fescue grass that covers the fairways and the rough. Depending on the time of year, the grasses may be tall and willowy or freshly mowed. Either way, fescue provides a lot of challenge to the golfer. A bad break into the rough, full of divots and coarse grass, makes it extremely hard to get a club around the ball and may leave the golfer feeling like he's landed in no-man's land. Like the classic rough and rugged Scottish courses that have served as the inspiration for this course's design, golfers face the challenge of playing against the elements and natural obstacles. Early tee times are best, as the winds really kick up by 3:00 or 4:00 P.M. If the winds are up, for example, you might need to use a 3-wood just to hit the 225-yard par 3 on 17.

There's no doubt that Dye's Whistling Straits courses are intended to bowl golfers over with their breathtakingly rugged terrain and that Dye has used these visual factors to mentally intimidate golfers. Dye is known for pushing the limits, but he also designs fairly. The seemingly precarious and tight holes allow room for mistakes, though in some cases that extra room may be hidden. The Irish Course's 13th hole is an example of one such blind spot. Though generous in size at 14,500 square feet, the green is obscured by the 20- to 40-foot dunes that surround it. I can see only about 10 percent to 25 percent of the putting surface from the tee I play, while only the flagstaff is visible from other tees! It's not only helpful to have a caddy direct play on the Straits; it's imperative. The Straits Course is a walking-only course, so caddies are, thankfully, provided.

The Irish Course does permit golf carts, so whether you opt for the modern convenience or choose to walk the 5 1/2 miles, your trek will take you through some

> A FEW YEARS
> AGO, I SHOT
> MY PERSONAL
> BEST ON
> THIS COURSE.

stunning features. In many ways, the Irish Course is an amalgam of the three other courses that comprise The American Club complex. There's plenty of water. Holes 2, 8, 11, 12, and 13 provide views of Lake Michigan. A 10 1/2-acre reservoir hugs the fairway on the left on holes 16 and 17. Four streams meander through the treed Irish Course and are traversed by ten wooden bridges. Bentgrass covers the fairways and greens, while fescue covers the rough. Very little manicuring is done to the rough, so similar natural obstacles exist in the mounds and berms as can be found on the Straits.

As impressive as Whistling Straits is, I must confess that my heart belongs to Blackwolf Run and the River Course in particular. A few years ago, I shot my personal best on this course. Perhaps these courses on Blackwolf Run carry a certain cachet for me because they feature the beautiful, well-crafted, and challenging holes that one has come to expect from Pete Dye, as well as constant reminders of their natural setting and the area's indigenous food and wildlife. The River Course is aptly named for the Sheboygan River, which hugs at least half of the holes on the course. The salmon run begins in late September and continues into late October. I was anxious to see the fish in action; however, Mike O'Reilly, the golf pro who accompanied me, cautioned me to proceed quickly through the 2nd hole because salmon routinely become caught in the dam there and create an unpleasant smell. I had to wonder if the hole's name, "Burial Mounds," bore any allusions to the plight of the fish; leave it to Pete Dye to design a hole using a golfer's sense of smell as a possible obstacle! Mike assured me that I would have a great opportunity to see the salmon at the 5th hole.

From the white tee on number 5, the 376-yard par 4 truly is "Made in Heaven." I teed off from the elevated tee box, mindful of the river and a large bunker to my right. My ball landed safely in the fairway not too far away from the bunker on the left. I soaked in the spectacular view. The fall foliage was phenomenal, and I did see the salmon running. Briefly, I worked my way down the embankment to observe a lone fly fisherman snag a fish. On my way back up to the fairway, I noticed some raspberries growing in the rough. I helped myself to a handful of the delicious, sun-ripened berries and continued on.

leaves covered much of the wooded grounds leading to the course. Then the wide-open expanse greeted me. There were geese in flight over magnificent meadows and Midwestern prairie. I joined up with Mike O'Reilly at the Log Cabin Clubhouse for another round together. Meadows characterize the front 9. It is peaceful and calming to be surrounded by the subtly rolling fairways and by prairie grasses and wildflowers in the rough. I made an apple tree food find on the 4th hole. Then on the 6th hole, I was faced with the tough 406-yard par 4—"Serpentine." Mike cautioned me to keep my ball on the left side of the fairway to shorten my approach but to stay out of the large bunkers on the left and the tall grass on the right. Once I navigated through the long S-curve, it was an easy pitch onto the large green.

...this is the best hole he has ever designed...

For me, and I would think for Dye since he has said that this is the best hole he has ever designed, the 9th is the course's signature hole. Target-style, at 297 yards, this is a short par 4 with a risk-and-reward format. Riskier play for long hitters would be to go for the green over the trees on the right. A safer approach calls for a shorter drive with a 4- or 5-iron; play it left of the trees, careful of the bunkers that flank the green. The River Course also features one of the most challenging finishing holes that I've played. There's waste area on the left that stretches the length of the hole but an open front green; drive your ball straight with everything that you've got left.

On the other side of the Sheboygan River is Meadow Valleys, Blackwolf Run's second 18-hole course. Golden

By contrast, the valley portion of the course on the back 9 is full of deep gullies and steep grade changes. Fourteen, a dogleg-right par 4, is a gorgeous hole, enhanced by the autumn splendor and the stream nearly surrounding the green located about 40 feet below. I needed all the help I could get on the next hole. Fifteen is called "Mercy." This is a tough par 3, and the day's back-pin position made it even tougher. Though the huge green is helpful and I did get my ball on, the deep swail that runs through it served as a launching pad for my ball to reverse direction, gain speed, and roll right off the edge's steep drop into a sea of tall grasses below. After searching unsuccessfully for my ball, Mike told me about the hole's well-used "exchange program." He explained it was not unusual

*Dramatic views of
Lake Michigan made
the Whistling Straits
courses a stunning
location for the 2004
PGA Championship.*

practice here to resort to replacing a lost ball with someone else's. I couldn't argue with his version of Midwestern gumption. I fared better on the next holes and even redeemed myself on "Maple Syrup" at 17. Maybe it was the food reference.

The day was coming to an end. The season's shortened days produced some glorious fingers of sunlight across the valley and deer that ventured out

for a few nibbles. The golf was just what I needed to clear my mind and reconnect to nature. Now I was primed to take full advantage of the spa's special treatment designed specifically for golfers and then to enjoy the culinary delights back at The American Club.

Peggy Smith greeted me and provided a brief tour of the facility. She explained that the Kohler Waters Spa focuses on water-based treatments, chosen as a means to highlight the many bath and plumbing products produced by Kohler Company and to complement the body's own primary element, water. Treatments mirror the evolution of the bath, ranging from a classic-style "Renaissance Bath" in a free-standing copper steeping tub to a futuristic "Sok Bath" in which you are treated to color and light therapy while enjoying the restorative effects of a cascading whirlpool. Other hydrotherapeutic treatments Peggy described are the Tsunami, the Still Waters body wrap, and Kohler's signature treatment that features all of the elements—the Riverbath. Approach the Riverbath by traversing a path of river rocks specially collected from the banks of Lake Superior before relaxing in front of a fire for a foot soak and neck massage. Rinse away a lime exfoliant for the body under a shower, and then slip into a bath that simulates river currents. Of course, a shower under a Kohler state-of-the-art fixture complements any treatment. After the intensive golf, I recommend the Golfer's Massage, then head for the Golfer's Foot Renewal. This is pure decadence. After a pedicure and foot massage; special self-heating mud is applied. By the time the treatment was completed, I felt like a new man.

I headed back to The American Club, energized and ready to explore my options for refreshing the palate. I took a peek into the Horse & Plow Tavern, whose menu features a wide variety of locally brewed beers by the bottle and on tap. I found just the spot to sample pairings of the fabulous artisanal cheeses made all around Wisconsin with an amazing offering of local microbrew beer at the Winery Bar located in the main hotel next to the Immigrant Room restaurant. The cozy, clubby atmosphere is very inviting. Just past the bistro-style bar, leather and plush overstuffed chairs and sofas beckon. Subdued lighting and luxurious wall tapestries complete the cozy atmosphere. The cheese cave located at the far end of the den-like space is the lounge's major feature. I had noticed this mouthwatering enticement through a window cut out from the castle-like, stone-lined passageway as I walked to the lounge and restaurant area. Separated by a wine-colored velvet curtain, the cheese cave is a revolving showplace for over 350 Wisconsin cheeses. Choose a cheese flight, with or without an accompanying wine flight, and take notes on the informative menu, or do as I did and enjoy your own selections paired with the local beer.

Executive Chef Rhys Lewis enthusiastically walked me through some of his favorite selections. On a butcher's block table, he sliced samples that had properly reached room temperature under their individual glass domes, allowing for the fullest of flavor and aroma. The wonderfully named Fat Squirrel, an amber nut-brown ale from the New Glarus Brewery,

APPROACH THE RIVERBATH BY TRAVERSING A PATH OF RIVER ROCKS SPECIALLY COLLECTED FROM THE BANKS OF LAKE SUPERIOR.

paired particularly well with the nutty components in the Grande Cru Surchoix Gruyère from Monroe, Wisconsin, and the butterscotch notes in the Marisa, a delicious extra-aged sheep's milk cheese from Mauston, Wisconsin. Trade Lake Cedar, from Grantsburg, Wisconsin, another sheep's milk cheese, earthy and robust with great mouth feel, made for an interesting pairing with a lambic-style beer called Belgian Red, also produced by the New Glarus Brewery. The tart, tawny-colored beer was redolent with Door County, Wisconsin, cherries.

I completed my flight thoroughly impressed with the range of cheese and beer that is currently in production in Wisconsin. In fact, I was quite taken by the exceptional quality and true craftsmanship of many of the cheeses and the New Glarus Brewery in particular. I began making inquiries about the whereabouts of this truly artisanal Wisconsin brewery. A detour to see this operation would be a fun adventure before returning to Chicago. Others share my sentiments about the locally produced food and beverages. The Kohler Food & Wine Experience, sponsored by *Food & Wine* magazine, is held here at The American Club every October. This weekend-long event features culinary demonstrations, tastings, and seminars given by nationally renowned chefs, wine and spirits experts, and restaurateurs. You don't want to miss an opportunity to attend this gala venue at the Kohler Design Center. This is a classic case of life imitating and becoming art. Where else can you sample superior food and drink while surrounded by enormous kitchen and bath fixtures?

I ended my stay at Kohler with a fine meal at the Immigrant Room. The atmosphere may not pack the dramatic wallop that the Kohler Food & Wine Experience carries, but it is decorated with evident care, which certainly contributes to and complements the very enjoyable dining experience. The restaurant is intimately divided into six rooms, each of which is decorated in a style indicative of an ethnic group that settled the area. The rooms feel sweet and playful, almost like a life-size dollhouse. For example, blue and white delftware adorns the wood hutches in the eighteenth-century-style Dutch Room, while antique walnut furnishings from Normandy fill the French Room. Every room has its own variety of fresh flowers to complete the effect. I was seated in the dark wood-paneled, red-wine room, separated from the adjoining dining rooms by wide pocket doors.

The friendly waitstaff are most attentive and definitely proud Green Bay Packers fans. I enjoyed a little football banter with my servers, and then the chef's tasting, which commenced with a beluga caviar course, followed by carrot soup with white truffle oil.

The salad course highlighted many foods of Wisconsin. A quenelle of local Gorgonzola and poached Asian pear slices paired beautifully with Neuske's bacon, black walnuts, and salad greens. Completing this seven-course feast, I reflected on the Ruskin quote I had noticed earlier and agreed that Kohler does live up to its high aspirations. Its credo, linking labor with art, is all-pervasive. By approaching work with the passion of an artist, work indeed does become like play. Enjoying the fruits of all of this passionate labor does feel like fun.

That element of playfulness and passionate work extends into many of the fine artisanal products from Wisconsin. Spurred on by the impressive examples of cheese and beer that I tried the day before, I decided to take the extra time to find New Glarus, Wisconsin, and its brewery. I headed off in the direction of Madison, Wisconsin's capital. If the lure of an awesome brewery is not reason enough to justify the trip to New Glarus, as it certainly was for me, the area boasts several other points of interest worth exploring. Located just outside of Madison, Cave of the Mounds, with its dramatic stalactite and stalagmite formations, is the most significant example of underground caverns in the Midwest. Or tour Frank Lloyd Wright's former home and school of architecture at Taliesin in nearby Spring Green, Wisconsin. The windy 25-mile drive from Madison also qualifies as a draw in my book. Quaint farms and well-maintained buildings dot the landscape of the little towns leading to New Glarus.

The town of New Glarus dubs itself "America's Little Switzerland." Founded as a Swiss colony in 1845,

the town is adorned with flags, banners, and shields colorfully representing various Swiss cantons. Swiss chalet-style buildings line the town's streets, while two musical clock towers fill the air with traditional songs. There are many restaurants that feature Swiss specialties like fondue, raclette, schnitzel, and rösti potatoes. I ducked into the cozy, wood-lined chalet called Glarner Stube on First Avenue and sank my teeth into a hearty and delicious bratwurst and sauerkraut sandwich. The accompanying mustard was quintessentially Swiss.

There are also many enticing delis, chocolate houses, and Swiss bakeries, as well as little shops that sell Swiss trinkets. When it came to taverns, Peumpel's felt undeniably authentic. Hand-painted murals depicting the original owner's hometown in Switzerland line the bar's walls. They have darkened over the years, but this simply adds to the sense of tradition that literally hangs in the air. Locals are still known to play the Swiss card game Yass, and several beers from the New Glarus Brewery are featured on tap here. I was getting closer and closer to my main objective—to meet the people of the New Glarus Brewery and see their operation—and my taste buds nearly drove me there themselves!

Owners Dan and Debbie Carey, an extremely friendly and unpretentious couple, couldn't have offered a warmer welcome. They walked me through an extensive tasting of their amazing beers and through a tour of their facility. For the Careys, everything is laid out for you to see; there are no smoke and mirror tricks. Their labor of love is true beer-making craftsmanship, proudly displayed in the open for all to observe. The Careys' operation is impressive, informative, and worth the detour.

Step into the Old World farmhouse that houses the Careys' brewery, through a small retail section, and then into their operation itself. Observe the machinery used for the mashing process. These two enormous gleaming copper kettles were personally dismantled from a defunct brewery in Bavaria and installed in the New Glarus Brewery by Dan Carey himself. Peek inside the lab where the yeast is grown and at the various barreling stations for aging and fermentation. Finally, enjoy a sampling of the Careys' various beers after finishing the tour in the packaging room, where the beer is bottled or poured into kegs.

A master brewer, Dan has enjoyed true accolades over the years, culminating in being awarded "Small Brewing Company Brewmaster of the Year" and the brewery being named "Small Brewing Company of the Year," both at the Great American Beer Festival in 2003. From the four-ton brewer's mill, the lager tanks where beer is aged, and the old merlot wood barrels used in the fruit beer's process of spontaneous fermentation, to the multitude of awards that have been bestowed on the Careys and their beers, everything in this facility is big!

I think part of the magic at the New Glarus Brewery, though, is the Careys' ability to manage all of this grandness with a human perspective. The family dog, a cavalier spaniel called Murphy, playfully roams the premises. Festive Champagne bottles containing the New Glarus Brewery's signature fruit beers are still hand-sealed with red Wisconsin cheesemaker's wax. The Careys clearly enjoy their life's work. I sensed the same philosophy at work here that I observed at The American Club. In fact, Dan and Debbie had just returned from a night's stay there. When I mentioned my memorable experience there, their eyes lit up and they nodded knowingly.

The pursuit of joie de vivre, a state of mind that too often eludes so many of us in our daily lives, is very much at work at the New Glarus Brewery and in every facet of The American Club. From the four stellar golf courses created by Pete Dye, a true artist of golf course design, to the hotel, spa, and culinary offerings at Kohler, the factory's original ethos continues to act as the driving force behind all that goes on in Kohler. I believe this atmosphere rubs off on those that come here. After all, I did shoot my personal best on one of these very courses. I take this passion back with me and find it spurs on my own work. I know it will infuse your daily labors as well.

WORK BECOMES PLAY

Kohler, Wisconsin

WATERCRESS SOUP

RATING: Par for the Course on a Par 3: Low Greens Fees

SERVES: 6

In the spring, watercress grows along the River Course in the shallow water near the banks of the Sheboygan River. The soup, with its rich green color and herbal notes, is restorative and fortifying. I enjoy a hearty bowl of this soup for lunch when the weather is brisk, or a small cupful as a first course to a larger meal. If fresh cress is out of season or unavailable in your area, try substituting sorrel or arugula.

1 small leek
2 bunches watercress
2 bunches celery leaves
1 small onion
1/4 cup (1/2 stick) butter
1 garlic clove
1 bay leaf
6 cups Vegetable Stock (page 181)
salt and freshly ground pepper to taste
1 teaspoon honey (optional)

Wash the leek, watercress, celery leaves and onion and cut into small pieces. Heat a saucepan with a few tablespoons of the butter. Add the chopped vegetables, garlic and bay leaf and sweat over low heat until the greens brighten but the vegetables are not brown.

Add enough Vegetable Stock to just cover the vegetables. Cook over medium heat until tender. Remove the garlic and bay leaf. Process the soup in a blender until smooth.

Season with salt and pepper. Add the remaining butter and the honey if the soup is bitter. Heat to serving temperature.

TIP: For a heartier rustic presentation, add an egg to the soup just before serving. Bring the soup to a boil and cook with the egg for 2 to 3 minutes. Your favorite cheese can be another delicious embellishment, or try a dollop of crème fraîche with a few drops of vinegar.

Trout with Coriander en Papillote

RATING: Par for the Course on a Par 4; Average Greens Fees

SERVES: 4

Lake Michigan waters often crash into the breakers along The Whistling Straights. At these times, the lake takes on a quality of a mighty ocean, while on other days the water is placid. In either state, the Great Lakes are teeming with many types of fish, including trout. This dish is simple enough to prepare, but there is a technical aspect—precision folding—that is crucial to its success. So, in this case, choose between your foil or parchment paper as you do your irons or woods.

2 tablespoons olive oil
1/2 cup chopped leeks
1/2 cup julienned carrots
4 trout, heads and bones removed
1 teaspoon coriander seeds
2 teaspoons herbes
    de Provence
salt and freshly ground
    pepper to taste
3/4 cup white wine

Preheat the oven to 425 degrees. Brush the olive oil on 4 squares of foil or baking parchment large enough to enclose the fish. Layer the leeks, carrots and trout on the squares. Season with coriander seeds, herbes de Provence, salt and pepper.

Fold half the foil or parchment over the trout and begin to close the packets by folding the edges over, adding the wine when the packets are partly sealed. Complete the folding to enclose the ingredients completely; the finished packets should look like the letter "D."

Place the packets in a baking pan and bake for about 12 minutes or until the fish is opaque and firm. Serve the trout from the opened packet or remove to serving plates.

TIP: Take care to fold the foil or parchment well; the secret to steaming en papillote is having a good seal. The olive oil will help seal the folded edge.

RUSTIC POTATO AND ONION LAYERS

RATING: Par for the Course on a Par 3; Low Greens Fees

SERVES: 6 to 8

Like so many European families who immigrated to Kohler, I keep comfort food dishes like this one, loaded with modest staples of potatoes and onions, in my cooking repertoire. It adds real backbone to a meal.

5 medium potatoes
2 medium onions
salt and freshly ground
   pepper to taste
2 slices bacon
1 bay leaf
1 to 2 cups Vegetable
   Stock (page 181)

Preheat the oven to 325 degrees. Cube the potatoes and slice the onions 1/8 inch thick. Place in separate bowls and season with salt and pepper.

Alternate layers of the potatoes and onions in a buttered baking dish, beginning and ending with potatoes. Top with the bacon slices and bay leaf. Add enough Vegetable Stock to reach 3/4 of the way up the side of the dish.

Bake for 45 minutes. Increase the oven temperature to 425 degrees and bake for 20 minutes longer; check for tenderness by piercing a potato with the tip of a knife. Discard the bay leaf before serving.

TIP: Make this dish ahead of time; its flavor and consistency will definitely improve.

RIVER COURSE HOLE #5 VENISON TENDERLOIN WITH RASPBERRIES

RATING: A Short Par 3; High Greens Fees

SERVES: 4

I use Raspberry Tart, the raspberry-style lambic beer from New Glarus Brewery, in this dish, but a sweet wine or another raspberry beer will produce a winning combination as well.

4 (6- to 8-ounce) pieces venison tenderloin
salt and freshly ground pepper to taste
1 tablespoon olive oil
1 cup raspberry beer
1 pint raspberries
1 to 3 tablespoons plain bread crumbs
4 teaspoons butter

Preheat the oven to 375 degrees. Season the venison on all sides with salt and pepper. Heat a sauté pan with the olive oil and add the venison. Sear on both sides for about 2 minutes. Remove the venison to a roasting pan and reserve at room temperature.

Add the beer to the sauté pan and stir to deglaze the pan. Cook until reduced by 1/4 and add the raspberries. Season with salt and pepper and cook for 2 minutes. Add enough bread crumbs to form a paste consistency and remove from the heat.

Spread the raspberry paste on the venison pieces and top each with a teaspoon of butter to keep the meat moist. Roast for 3 to 4 minutes for medium-rare.

BRAISED ENDIVE IN PORT

RATING: A Short Par 3; High Greens Fees

SERVES: 4

Braised endive is a great accompaniment to venison, as its flavors give balance to the fruit-based components in the main course dish. The wilted leaves of endive in their various shades of purple feel like autumn.

4 whole heads endive
2 tablespoons butter
1/4 cup Vegetable Stock (page 181)
1/2 cup port
1 or 2 tablespoons sugar

Cut the endive heads into halves lengthwise. Remove the hearts and ends and cut into thirds lengthwise.

Melt the butter in a saucepan and add the endive. Sweat over medium-low heat for 2 minutes. Add the Vegetable Stock and cook until nearly all the liquid has been reduced.

Add the wine and cook for about 15 minutes or until the endive is tender, adding the sugar during the last few minutes of cooking time if the endive tastes bitter.

TIP: Place the heel of a loaf of bread on top of the endive while it is braising. The bread will help to remove any bitterness from the flavor.

PEAR AND RAISIN CHUTNEY

RATING: Par for the Course on a Par 3; Average Greens Fees

MAKES: 4 cups

Chutney is so versatile. I like to serve it as an accompaniment to a selection of Wisconsin cheeses. Chutney is also a natural pairing for pork, chicken, and veal dishes. It is a great condiment to have on hand.

3 firm pears, chopped
1 cup golden raisins
1 large white onion, chopped
1/3 cup coarsely chopped candied ginger
1 cup white vinegar
1/3 cup honey
1 teaspoon chili powder
1 teaspoon salt

Combine the pears, raisins, onion and ginger in a saucepan. Add the vinegar, honey, chili powder and salt and mix well.

Cook over medium-low heat for 45 minutes or until the ingredients are tender and most of the liquid has evaporated.

Cool to room temperature and spoon into a storage container. Store in the refrigerator.

STRAWBERRY AND CRANBERRY AU GRATIN SABAYON

RATING: A Short Par 4; High Greens Fees

Serves 4

An elegant last course, this dessert is redolent of Champagne and the natural sweetness of the dried and fresh berries. Choose fresh fruit at its peak of ripeness. If strawberries are unavailable, try an alternative fruit that is in season. By all means, fill your Champagne flutes with the remaining bubbly and toast to the joys of living!

1/2 cup Champagne
20 strawberries, hulled and cut into quarters
1/4 cup dried cranberries
5 egg yolks
4 teaspoons sugar

Bring the Champagne to a boil in a small saucepan. Remove from the heat immediately and add the strawberries and cranberries. Let stand to steep.

Combine the egg yolks and sugar in a mixing bowl. Whip with a balloon whisk attachment at medium-high speed for 10 minutes or until the mixture is pale and thick and forms a ribbon from the whisk.

Strain the berry mixture, reserving the Champagne and the fruit. Place the fruit in 4 individual ramekins or shallow gratin dishes.

Add the reserved Champagne gradually to the egg mixture, mixing constantly at medium speed. Increase the speed and beat until the mixture is smooth and foamy.

Preheat the broiler to high. Spoon the egg mixture over the fruit in the prepared ramekins. Place under the broiler and broil for 1 minute or until the top is golden brown.

From food to golf,
there is something
for everyone in
Northeast Florida.

Panelli

THE PLACE FOR EVERY PLAYER

FLORIDA

Ponte Vedra & Amelia Island

While some of my travel destinations are subject to the ever-changing seasons, which affect the area's terrain and golf course conditions, the availability of certain foods, and the accessibility to stay and play at the resort, there are few surprises in Northeast Florida. You can be sure of a pleasant, temperate climate, golf courses in peak condition, an abundance of local seafood and tropical produce, and truly warm and friendly people. Like the saying goes, there really is something for everyone here in Northeast Florida.

I arrived at the Jacksonville airport on a late-August evening and began the 30-mile drive to Ponte Vedra Beach, Florida, for a planned stay at the Sawgrass Marriott Resort & Beach Club.

As a guest of the Sawgrass Marriott, I was welcome to enjoy playing their two Tournament Players Club golf courses, more commonly known as the TPC Stadium and the TPC Valley Courses, which are otherwise private. Though I had the TPC Stadium Course on my mind and was looking forward to an early morning tee time with Cindy Reid, the course pro and director of instruction, I had to face the fact that Murphy's Law applies in Northeast Florida, as it does anywhere. An uninvited guest had also shown up, threatening to clear out the golf courses: dreaded rain had started to fall.

I inquired at the concierge desk about alternative activities for the morning should the rain persist. The friendly staff was most helpful. They directed me to St. Augustine, Florida, America's oldest permanently settled European city. In addition to spending a morning exploring St. Augustine's historic component and having an opportunity to sip from the legendary spring of Ponce de León's Fountain of Youth, I could still get my golf fix! St. Augustine is also home to the World Golf Hall of Fame & IMAX Theater at World Golf Village. The Marriott staff showed real enthusiasm for the museum's in-depth coverage of golf's greatest, urging me not to miss the opportunity to feel like a pro by attempting a winning putt under simulated high-pressure conditions, with crowd noise and the presence of television cameras. Either way, rain or shine, I looked forward to a day filled with golf and adventure.

As luck would have it, I awoke to a cloudless sky. After a quick breakfast in the café, I caught a shuttle to the nearby golf course, where I was scheduled to meet with Cindy. As we rode to the first hole, Cindy, a seven-year veteran of the LPGA, gave me a little background on herself, as well as on the TPC Stadium Course at Sawgrass. The first of its kind, conceived by then-PGA Tour Commissioner Deane Beman and designer Pete Dye, the distinctive tiered knolls surrounding each hole of the TPC Stadium Course have revolutionized golf-course design, as well as the interaction between players and spectators.

Prior to the first Players Championship, in 1982, most major golf championships were played on private courses that were not accessible to the general public. By opening its doors, the TPC Stadium Course provides fans access to front-row seats from which they can truly appreciate professional tournaments, and average players like me can now play a championship course. The distinctive grassed grandstands that surround the stage-like greens reinforce this blurring of the boundaries between professional and avid golfers, creating the sense of giving a performance; you can feel a bit like a star if you allow your imagination to run wild.

After watching Cindy tee off, my illusion was quickly shattered. There was no question who was the pro and who was the eager pupil. With its angular fairways and small, undulating greens, this 6,950-yard, par-72 course demanded controlled, exacting shots. Unlike in March, when the Players Championship takes place, the wind was not a factor. Cindy and I made our way through the front 9. I caught sight of the occasional jumping fish or an alligator poking his head out of the water. The heavy air and heat made for a lazy day for the surrounding wildlife, but my excitement and anticipation was steadily mounting, for I knew what awaited me on the back 9.

The Island hole, at the 17th, arguably one of the most famous—or infamous—holes in golf, depending on whose vantage point you consider, was such an allure. We played through hole 11, Cindy's favorite hole, a par 5, and the scenic 13th hole. I remembered seeing hole 13, which looks out to a waterfall from the green, while I ate breakfast. The challenging pin positioning on this par 3 was down on the left, making it tough to navigate through all of the green's many undulations. Cindy's tip to play it smart here could not help me on the ill-fated 17th hole.

Cindy's advice to aim for the middle of the green was sound for an amateur like myself; the various undulations that are present all along the green's perimeter are just as tricky to navigate as the approach shot. The par-3, 134-yard 17th hole proved to be one of my day's highlights and my most humbling hole. Cindy advised me to grab my 7-iron. After my seventh attempt hit the water, Cindy shared a comforting statistic with me. Each year it is estimated that between 120,000 and 150,000 balls are recovered from the water at this hole alone! Despite my first seven attempts, I took comfort in the fact that I was in good company and gained real motivation from the Freddie Couples story.

For several years running at the Players Championship, Couples sank his first ball in the water at the 17th, only to nail his second shot right into the hole! Standing at the tee, I could sense how much this stadium design has impacted the game of golf and the real effect a crowded tier of fans has upon a player in a competition like the Players Championship, which holds the biggest purse of all the Majors. Couples' heroic clutch play did inspire me. I hit my eighth ball solidly onto the middle right of the green, and in two more strokes, I finished the hole. The Sunday pin placement on the green's back right was a foot lower than the rest of the green. Thankfully, my ball placement did not add any more difficulty to a most frustrating but truly memorable hole.

While waiting for the shuttle back to the hotel, I chatted with one of the caddies, a native to the area. I asked for his recommendation for a crab shack that the locals truly love. I was looking for a bit of local flavor to go along with the area's fine seafood. He unequivocally recommended the Outback Crab Shack. The restaurant is located off County Road 13 North, just a 15-minute drive from St. Augustine. I dropped off my clubs at the hotel and jumped into the car for a culinary adventure. The area quickly changed to an established, rural environment. I couldn't miss the restaurant. Its parking lot was full of cars and motorcycles, and the massive dock in the back along the banks of the St. Johns River was lined with boat after boat. The live music filling the air gave this place a sense of ease and welcome.

Owner Joe Tuttle showed me what real hospitality is all about. He whisked me off to a great table under a gazebo that overlooks the water and one of its many alligators, who popped his head out from time to time. A friendly waitress returned with my beer and a couple of extras nicely iced in a bucket. It was hard to decide between the incredible options. I was leaning toward the local catch, but it was hard to narrow the field with so many choices: crab cakes, soft-shell or hard-shell blue crabs, shrimp, clams, fillets of fish smoked on the premises, or fried alligator. Being the gourmand that he undoubtedly is, Joe understood my dilemma and solved it, bringing me an amazing platter that featured each local specialty.

The alligator was a dining first for me, and I thoroughly enjoyed the delicate white meat, deep-fried to a perfect golden crispness. The Outback's breading was equal to the sweetness of the local seafood. The light batter was seasoned to balance, not overpower, its prized interior. I can only describe my experience here as a feast. Though Joe's restaurant is not fancy, this wide-ranging culinary extravaganza ranks up there with four- and five-star dining establishments. The ambience is perfect, the service is flawlessly attentive, and the Outback Crab Shack has the ability to turn out many delicious and well-prepared foods. The simple, unadorned setting is really the only criterion differentiating Joe's Outback Crab Shack from a more upscale dining experience.

Joe's first objective is to make his patrons feel comfortable. He's more than willing to give the novice a lesson in how to shell a blue crab. He's also a very generous restaurateur who truly gives back to his community. Each Thanksgiving, he opens his doors to the public for a free feast; he invites his guests to bring a side dish if they wish. My mind raced considering the culinary possibilities for the Thanksgiving turkey. Joe's tangerine and orange wood-filled smoker must make a really succulent and flavorful bird. If you must be away from home on this holiday, I can't think of a friendlier place to spend Thanksgiving.

As I was leaving the Outback Crab Shack, I couldn't help drawing a parallel between the openness and inclusiveness that characterized both my morning golf and my dining experience. I hope you will seek out these special places, and they will become the backdrops to your own priceless memories.

I returned to Ponte Vedra Beach and finished my day with a walk along the Atlantic Ocean and a sunset cocktail at the nearby Ponte Vedra Lodge's beachfront lounge. The AAA-5-Diamond Ponte Vedra Inn & Club evokes the same relaxed elegance that characterizes the area. The clean ocean breeze carried a light scent of fresh oysters. I love to soak in the sights and smells of the ocean. It was a sort of final feast for my senses, as I concluded my first full day in Northeast Florida. My round of golf at The TPC Stadium Course and the day's ensuing activities really lived up to my hopes for a one-of-a-kind experience.

I began the next day by driving to Amelia Island, Florida, which is located off the northeastern tip of Florida on the Atlantic Ocean, just 33 miles north of Jacksonville. My one-hour drive from Ponte Vedra Beach took me across the Intracoastal Waterway and several other barrier islands. Though the southern part of the

> THE ALLIGATOR WAS A FIRST FOR ME, AND I THOROUGHLY ENJOYED THE DELICATE WHITE MEAT.

island offers several resort options, I settled on historic Fernandina Beach and the easy-going, quaint but funky feel of a little community and one of its charming bed-and-breakfasts, the Ash Street Inn.

My hosts, Jill Dorson Chi and Sam Chi, greeted me with a friendly welcome and a refreshing glass of homemade lemonade. They showed me around the adjoining buildings, which were built in 1888 and 1904, each featuring lovingly maintained examples of period furnishings. The Victorian charm, from the overhead porch fans in the building's open veranda to the parlor and dining room with an arts-and-crafts tiled fireplace and carved breakfront, created a relaxing environment that was anything but stuffy. The spacious and immaculately kept rooms balanced the turn-of-the-century style with modern amenities. I sat outdoors at the pool near a small arbor, chatting with Jill and Sam. Their story is an interesting one.

Former sports writers based out of San Francisco, the young couple's schedules kept them frequently on the road, oftentimes literally crossing flight paths in the night as each traveled to his or her next professional football or golf event. Still writing as freelancers, Sam and Jill explained that they enjoyed the opportunity to remain in one place as a vested part of a community to nurture a historic property and the guests who visit. Amelia Island answers all of these points plus provides a temperate year-round climate for enjoying the miles of sand-dune beaches and excellent golf. After they had entertained me with some great anecdotal stories about their professional sportswriting experiences over the years, we got down to the very serious business of discussing our golf handicaps and the golf options on Amelia Island.

The Chis listed five golfing options on the island. I asked for their personal endorsements, and without a moment's pause, Sam and Jill responded in unison with The Golf Club at North Hampton. So I filled my afternoon with a round of golf at the three-year-old course designed by Arnold Palmer. A par-72, 5,872-yard course from the white tee, this course is a real gem. The personality of the front 9 is characterized by a woodland setting, whereas the back 9 made me think of an old Scottish links course. I enjoyed the contrast between the rough dunes littered with mature tufts of saw grass and the finely manicured tees, fairways, and greens. Here, the traditional links meet with the unique topography of Northern Florida. On the 1st hole, a par 4, I aimed for the middle of the green to avoid the bunker on the right and out-of-bounds play on the left. I remained consistent and managed a par score, but knowing the risk-and-reward attitude that so characterizes the King, himself, and the courses that Palmer designs, I felt compelled to play a little on the edge. The next hole, a very challenging par 5, seemed to invite this aggressive approach. While considering my second shot, I could see that ball placement to the left center of the fairway would provide the best angle to the green. From here I decided to let it rip to get onto the green for a possible birdie or even the elusive eagle. With bunkers to the right and front of the green, I knew I was flirting with disaster. I pulled my approach shot just left of the green onto the first cut. I did not get the birdie I hoped for; my chip left me too challenging a putt, which came up just short of the hole. But the par score felt pretty good, and the calculated risks felt worthwhile.

The 11th hole is noteworthy for its dramatic 50-foot drop from the tee box to the fairway. From here I could view five other holes on the course, including holes 16 and 17. The 16th hole proved to be the most challenging, but there was plenty of room long and left of the green, so I played this one safe. The 17th was a different story. The large putting surface on this short par 3 finally yielded the reward birdie for which I hoped. I finished my round on a high and drove my cart back through the sandy trails to the clubhouse.

Back at the inn, I relaxed with one of my favorite beverages, the Arnold Palmer, which is made up of equal parts lemonade and iced tea. A fitting end to a great day of golf, it really is amazing how often the worlds of golf and food overlap! Once refreshed, I strolled through the historic part of Fernandina Beach. The island's telling nickname, The Isle of Eight Flags, alludes to the eight times it has changed hands—from the Native Americans, to France, to Spain, to Great Britain, to Mexico, to a Scotsman, and briefly to the Confederates during the Civil War—before finally coming under the United States' permanent jurisdiction in 1862. Though the island does have a lively past, I noticed examples of the Victorian era most strongly during my walk through town. I passed several landmarks of historic and architectural importance.

What I was really looking for was a great place to dine. There are some fine options if you are searching for local specialties. The Florida House is a 20-room boarding house with a courtyard in the back, where an all-you-can-eat Southern feast is served. They are known especially for their fried chicken. A sweet, yellow clapboard cottage nearby also drew me in. The owners of this restaurant, Le Clos, hail from none other than my native area of Provence. These were tempting options; however, I decided to trust my host's recommendation to eat at Joe's 2nd Street Bistro. I was seated outdoors on the upper gallery, where I could look out and enjoy the sights of historic Fernandina Beach. Joe's showed impeccable service, and its menu featured many local

> IT REALLY IS AMAZING HOW OFTEN THE WORLDS OF GOLF AND FOOD OVERLAP.

ingredients. I'm drawn to local fare because, for me, local means fresh. The flavors and quality of local foods can also really shine because this food does not have to survive a long voyage to get to your table. Fruits and vegetables can be harvested at their prime; seafood does not have to be frozen.

I selected the gray grouper from the list of fresh catches on the nightly specials. That particular day, Joe's was serving the grouper sautéed in a saffron broth with fennel, tomato, and leek. Very much like a bouillabaisse, it came served with saffron aïoli croustades. I sipped from my glass of fumé blanc and watched the sun set over the Fernandina Marina.

All of this wonderfully fresh and flavorful seafood made me want to explore the local industries. I met up with Captain Jeff Barksdale at the Fernandina Marina the next morning. I explained that I was interested in learning more about the local shrimping industry. Captain Jeff offered me a tour of the nearby barrier islands on his 42-foot sailing catamaran, *Island Time*, and guaranteed that we would find some shrimp boats to tail just a few miles out. I jumped at the chance.

Captain Jeff is a wealth of information. As we neared Cumberland Island, he pointed out a few wild horses. There are over 200 currently living on the island—all descendants of horses that escaped sinking Spanish ships that were under siege by pirates over 200 years ago. He also pointed out archaeological points of interest. I really liked this guy's humor. He told me that, before he knew its proper name, he called the rosetta spoonbill that we saw on the water's edge a "flamingrette" because of its pink and fluffy plumage. I don't know much about ornithology, but I do know that

this bird's pink color comes from its steady diet of shrimp. I was ready to live the *vie en rose* myself, so we headed for the shrimp boats visible in the distance.

We caught up to the *Margaret Lucille* just as she began pulling up her nets, which was quite a show. Captain Jeff explained that a small test net indicates the quantity of the catch. Once this net shows a satisfactory yield, the larger nets can be slowly raised. A group of dolphins playfully followed the nets. There was even a baby among the group. The special nets that these local shrimp boats use act as an attraction for the dolphins, as they provide an easy meal—more like a feeding frenzy!

Located at the net's midpoint is the net's special feature, called a turtle excluder. In addition to safely freeing any sea turtles that may get caught up, the excluder also kicks out fish and about a third of the shrimp catch. Use of these special nets shows a real sensitivity to the plight of endangered sea turtles; however, this method of shrimping does make it harder to compete with foreign product at market. Farmed Asian shrimp have driven the price of shrimp down to 1970s prices. So, while the local shrimp boats are mindful of the wildlife, they are becoming an endangered species themselves. Captain Jeff has noted a marked decrease in shrimp boats working in the waters off Amelia Island and feels that the days of a once-vital industry are dangerously numbered.

As I continued to watch the yellow slicker-clad crew on the *Margaret Lucille* pull up her nets, I made a pledge to myself that I would personally make a point to purchase shrimp caught from the wild, as opposed to the farmed variety, whenever possible. Besides the obvious advantage of superior flavor, I want to show my support of this industry. My hope is that as a true connoisseur of all the best things that life offers us, you will also treat yourself to the best-quality foods and help sustain the industries that bring these delicacies to our tables.

We watched the crew do an initial sorting by size on deck before dropping their nets for another run. They caught two types of shrimp. The white shrimp are distinctive for their bright shells, while the brownies are recognizable by their distinctive brown shells. I was eager to take some of this shrimp back with me so I could sample the sweet flavor that Captain Jeff raved about. As I left the boat and thanked the captain for an invigorating and memorable morning, he urged me to try the Blue Seas on Fletcher Avenue for the best battered local shrimp.

Just as the caddie from the TPC Stadium Course steered me toward his favorite place to eat, Captain Jeff confirmed that Northeast Floridians really are proud of and willing to share their special local places with anyone who shows an interest. This time, though, I wanted to do the cooking.

I returned to the Ash Street Inn and asked Sam and Jill if I could use their kitchen to cook my fresh shrimp. They were most obliging. I found a couple of mangoes in their kitchen, so I made a poaching liquid to cook the shrimp and a quick mango salsa as an accompaniment. In just a few minutes, the three of us sat under the breezy fans on the porch to enjoy the light lunch. It was my way of saying thank you for a most enjoyable time spent on Amelia Island.

It was nearly time to check out and head back to Jacksonville for my flight home. The time spent in Florida had indeed been a respite. It wasn't hard to relax and feel a part of Northeast Florida. Like the warm, gentle breezes that blow off the ocean, the locals were quick to whisk me into the mix. They freely offered helpful suggestions for their favorite places to dine on local specialties. These restaurants, whether they were ultracasual or more refined, were never short on friendly and colorful ambience. I give the golf experience a high rating as well. For an avid golfer like myself, having the opportunity to play The Golf Club at North Hampton Course, designed by Arnold Palmer, one of golf's all-time greats, and the TPC Stadium Course, a classic in its own right, was like being given two incredible treats. I will savor these memories—the sweet ones like the birdie on the 17th at North Hampton and even the bittersweet ones like the 17 I scored on the Stadium Course's Island Hole. The TPC Course gave me a run for my money, so to speak, but I'll look forward to trying my hand on this course again sometime. I urge you to make a trip to this part of Florida. Whether or not your handicap is like mine, the courses are open to all levels of play, and the people you will encounter on and off the course will make you feel most welcome.

CRAB CAKES WITH GRILLED SOFT-SHELL CRABS

RATING: A Short Par 3; High Greens Fees

SERVES: 4 with 3 small crab cakes each

Joe Tuttle's bountiful servings at his Outback Crab Shack were the inspiration behind this mouth-watering dish featuring soft-shell crabs and their crab cake cousins. As a complement to your own style of crab cake, pair a crispy cake with a bed of lettuce topped with a Ravigote Dressing (page 177) and crispy leeks, or pair a softer cake with fried vegetable chips. If soft-shell crabs are out of season or unavailable, just serve the crab cakes alone and no one will be the wiser.

1 pound crab meat, cleaned
2 eggs
1/2 cup finely ground bread crumbs
2 tablespoons chopped chives
1 tablespoon chopped shallot
1 teaspoon crushed garlic
2 teaspoons chopped cilantro
2 teaspoons Old Bay seasoning
1/4 to 1/2 cup heavy cream
3 tablespoons butter
2 soft-shell crabs, cleaned
salt and freshly ground pepper to taste

Preheat the grill; preheat the oven to 400 degrees. Combine the crab meat, eggs, bread crumbs, chives, shallot, garlic, cilantro and Old Bay seasoning in a bowl; mix well. Add enough cream to bind the mixture. Shape into 12 balls and press each ball into a 2 1/2-inch cake.

Heat the butter in an ovenproof skillet. Sauté the crab cakes in the butter until brown and crisp on both sides. Place in the oven and bake for 2 minutes to finish.

Sprinkle the soft-shell crabs with salt and pepper to taste. Grill for 1 minute on each side. Cut each crab into halves. To serve, top 3 crab cakes with a grilled soft-shell crab.

TIP: Crab cakes are best when their crispness suits one's personal preference. Sautéing in plain butter will certainly do the job; however, if you prefer your crab cake to have a crispy exterior, use clarified butter, as it reaches a higher temperature before burning—higher than many oils. It will therefore achieve the desired degree of crispness.

POACHED SHRIMP

RATING: A Short Par 3; High Greens Fees

SERVES: 4

Pair the poached shrimp with Mango Salsa (page 103) and enjoy a little taste of Amelia Island, Florida. The sweet and delicate flavor of fresh local shrimp needs little enhancement, so the poaching liquid—flavored with shrimp shells to simulate salty seawater—is more like a comfortable natural habitat in which the shrimp can cook.

24 medium shrimp in the shell
5 parsley stems
2 teaspoons coriander seeds
1 teaspoon fennel seeds

1 bay leaf
2 or 3 star anise
2 teaspoons peppercorns

Clean and butterfly the shrimp, leaving the tails intact and reserving the shrimp shells. Combine the parsley stems, coriander seeds, fennel seeds, bay leaf, star anise and peppercorns in a saucepan. Add just enough water to cover the reserved shrimp shells and bring to a boil.

Add the shrimp and remove from the heat. Let stand for 3 to 5 minutes or until the shrimp are opaque. Drain and serve warm or plunge into an ice water bath to cool if you prefer to serve them chilled.

TIP: Serve Poached Shrimp around the edge of a chilled martini glass of Mango Salsa.

GREEN SALAD WITH WARM GOAT CHEESE CROUTONS

RATING: Par for the Course on a Par 4; Average Greens Fees

SERVES: 4

This salad is a childhood favorite, and with one bite of the delicate greens and creamy goat cheese, I am immediately transported back to Provence. Adding the pecans allows me to give the dish an American flair— celebrating the best of both my worlds!

8 (1/4-inch) slices baguette or other bread
2 tablespoons olive oil
salt and freshly ground pepper to taste
1/2 cup Toasted Pecans (page 175)

1/4 cup olive oil
4 ounces goat cheese
mixed baby greens
4 to 6 teaspoons Balsamic Vinaigrette (page 176)

Preheat the oven to 350 degrees. Drizzle the bread slices with 2 tablespoons olive oil and season with salt and pepper. Arrange on a baking sheet and toast until light brown.

Spread the Toasted Pecans on a plate; pour 1/4 cup olive oil into a shallow bowl. Shape the goat cheese into 8 flat cakes just slightly smaller than the croutons.

Dip each cake into the olive oil and coat 1 side with the pecans. Place the cheese pecan side up on the croutons. Arrange on a baking sheet and place in the refrigerator for 1 hour to firm up.

Season the greens with salt and pepper in a bowl. Add the Balsamic Vinaigrette and toss to coat well.

Preheat the broiler to 400 degrees. Broil the croutons for 4 to 6 minutes or until the cheese is heated through. Serve 2 croutons on each salad serving.

MANGO SALSA

RATING: Par for the Course on a Par 3; Average Greens Fees

SERVES: 4

Mango Salsa benefits from a little time spent macerating in the refrigerator to infuse the flavors. It's the perfect do-ahead dish.

2 mangoes
3 medium tomatoes
1 small red onion
1 jalapeño chile (optional)

1/4 cup chopped parsley
1/2 cup olive oil
1/4 cup red wine vinegar
salt and freshly ground pepper to taste

Peel and chop the mangoes and place in a bowl. Seed and chop the tomatoes and add them to the mangoes. Chop the onion and add it to the mango mixture. Mince the jalapeño chile and add to the mangoes with the parsley, olive oil and vinegar. Season with salt and pepper and mix well.

Chill in the refrigerator for at least 1 hour or until serving time.

TIP: Chop the mangoes and tomatoes into the same size pieces to make for an attractive presentation.

PECAN-CRUSTED POMPANO WITH "SWAMP CABBAGE"

RATING: Par for the Course on a Par 4; Average Greens Fees

SERVES: 4

When I think of Florida and great food, my thoughts always turn to pompano. A variation of this fish preparation was a favorite of my customers when I worked in Boca Raton. My recent addition of hearts of palm to this dish was a serendipitous one, as I came to learn that the cabbage palm tree is Florida's official state tree. Hearts of palm, or "swamp cabbage," as I have heard it called by some locals near Ponte Vedra Beach, is the edible inner portion of the stem of the cabbage palm tree.

4 pompano fillets	*2 cups chopped seeded tomatoes*
3/4 cup milk	*7 slices bacon, crisp-cooked and chopped*
1/2 cup all-purpose flour	*1 (15-ounce) can hearts of palm,*
1/2 cup ground pecans or walnuts	*sliced 1/4 inch thick*
salt and freshly ground pepper to taste	*2 to 3 tablespoons butter*
2 tablespoons olive oil	

Combine the fish fillets with the milk in a bowl, coating well. Mix the flour, pecans, salt and pepper in a shallow dish. Remove the fish from the seasoned milk, reserving the milk. Coat the fish with the pecan mixture, gently shaking off any excess.

Heat 1 tablespoon of the olive oil in a sauté pan. Add the fish and sauté for 1 to 2 minutes on each side. Remove the fish to a plate to rest; drain and reserve the pan.

Heat the remaining tablespoon of olive oil in a second sauté pan and add the tomatoes. Sauté for 2 minutes to remove the excess moisture, then stir in the bacon and hearts of palm.

Add the reserved seasoned milk to the reserved sauté pan. Add the butter and whisk until foamy. Stir 1 spoonful of the foamy butter mixture into the hearts of palm mixture and arrange the fish fillets over the top. Adjust the seasoning and cook until heated through.

Spoon the vegetable mixture onto serving plates and top with the fish. Drizzle the remaining foamy butter mixture over the top.

TIP: Just as any conscientious golfer keeps his or her golf bag in good order, with each club in its proper place, this dish requires a well organized *mise en place*. Before beginning to cook, make sure that all ingredients are ready and organized in logical order. Then the quick preparation will be a snap, and you will be cooking like a pro.

GRILLED SWORDFISH WITH BELL PEPPER AND TOMATO COMPOTE

RATING: A Short Par 3; Average Greens Fees

SERVES: 4

This is a great dish to prepare with guests. While a twosome is out grilling the fish, the other pair can prepare the compote. In a short time, the dish can be ready and the group free to enjoy a relaxing evening at the 19th hole.

Bell Pepper and Tomato Compote

1/4 cup olive oil
2 Vidalia onions, chopped
4 red, yellow or orange bell peppers, seeded
   and chopped
2 tomatoes, seeded and chopped
1 garlic clove, chopped
1 thick slice prosciutto di Parma, finely chopped

Swordfish and Marinade

1/2 cup olive oil
2 teaspoons soy sauce
1 garlic clove, chopped
1 tablespoon coriander seeds
freshly ground pepper to taste
4 swordfish steaks
4 pats of butter
1 tablespoon coarsely chopped parsley,
   for garnish

For the compote, heat the olive oil in a sauté pan. Add the onions and sauté over medium heat until translucent. Add the bell peppers and sauté until tender. Add the tomatoes. Reduce the heat and cook for 8 to 10 minutes. Add the garlic and prosciutto and cook for 5 minutes longer.

For the swordfish and marinade, combine the olive oil, soy sauce, garlic, coriander seeds, and pepper in a bowl and mix well. Add the swordfish, coating well. Marinate in the refrigerator.

Preheat the grill to medium heat. Drain the swordfish and place on the grill; discard the marinade. Grill for 2 minutes. Rotate the fish 45 degrees and grill for 2 minutes longer. Turn the fish over and top with the butter to ensure moistness. Grill until done to taste.

Spoon the compote onto a serving platter. Arrange the swordfish on the compote and garnish with the parsley.

TIP: Rotating the fish 45 degrees on the grill before turning it over creates an attractive X marking. For an impressive presentation, serve the swordfish with the grill marks showing.

Lemon Tart

RATING: A Long Par 4; Average Greens Fees

SERVES: 8

It is hard not to get in a sunny mood after savoring this tart. Its clean citrus punch is mellowed by its buttery component. This makes for a decadent finish to a meal or pure satisfaction for an afternoon treat.

½ cup freshly squeezed lemon
   juice, seeds removed
1½ cups sugar
4 eggs
grated zest of ½ of a lemon
1 cup (2 sticks) plus 1 tablespoon
   butter, chopped
1 baked tart shell of Pâte Sucrée
   (page 187)

Combine the lemon juice, sugar, eggs and lemon zest in a double boiler and whisk until smooth. Place over hot water and cook until the mixture thickens and reaches 140 degrees, whisking constantly.

Whisk in the butter gradually and cook until emulsified. Place plastic wrap directly on the surface of the mixture and chill in the refrigerator.

Spoon the lemon filling into the baked tart shell to serve.

TIP: Coat the pastry shell with a thin layer of egg wash made of egg yolk, cream and sea salt toward the end of the baking time. This will seal the dough and protect it from moisture.

Whenever I tell someone that I am planning to travel to New York City for a golf and culinary adventure, the response is usually a very puzzled expression. It's not a failure to comprehend my desire to soak in the city's veritable cornucopia of eateries ranging from street food to some of the best fine dining to be had anywhere; it's the golf that confuses people. Not many people living outside of the New York City area, not even some of the city's own residents, are aware of the fact that the oldest public golf course in North America sits just a stone's throw away from the hustle and bustle of "the city that never sleeps."

UNCOVERING ITS
HIDDEN GEMS
NEW YORK

New York

The Ritz-Carlton in Battery Park
is a AAA 5-Diamond hotel located
near many points of interest,
including the ferry to Ellis Island.

While I worked as chef de cuisine at Trouvaille and then at La Goulue in New York City some years ago, I had the good fortune to discover Van Cortlandt Park Golf Course in the Bronx. For me, Van Cortlandt is more than just a public golf course. The stress from my hectic, busy days and nights working in the restaurants simply evaporated when I played Van Cortlandt. The course was just a subway ride away or a short drive from Manhattan, but I always felt that I had really gotten away from city life. The densely treed course features a large natural lake, plenty of wildlife, and well-manicured mature grounds. After a round of golf at Van Cortlandt, you will be energized and ready to hit the pavement in search of more of the city's hidden gems.

Start in the heart of Midtown with the perfect foil to a hotel that looks and runs like a beautiful piece of machinery. Enter off the 56th or 57th Street side between 6th and 7th Avenues to find the nameless, obscurely accessible, little burger joint that survives solely by word-of-mouth advertising just off the hotel's lobby. Pass a small desk in the lobby and look up to catch the only clue that you are about to stumble into a throwback burger joint in the middle of Manhattan. The neon sign overhead features no words—only a big, juicy burger depicted in multihued brightness. Proceed through the velvet curtain into a single room featuring rickety tables and chairs, a few dark booths, and faux-wood laminate walls, one of which is covered in napkin "artwork" provided by happy patrons bestowing their rave reviews and accolades upon the great grub.

When I visited, I approached the counter and noticed a cardboard sign stating "order here" and "cash only." The menu was so simple: burger or cheeseburger, fries, soda, beer, brownies, and shakes after 3 P.M. My choices were few, but that is the beauty of this place! So I placed my order for a cheeseburger, fries, and soda with Andy, a very affable short-order cook. At $5 for the burger and $1.50 for the fries, I had to pause for a moment to fully appreciate the value at this posh Midtown location, especially when I considered that the price was competitive with the burger chains that litter nearly every neighborhood around the country.

I grabbed the basket containing my burger wrapped neatly in paper, my drink, and the tall cup of crispy, well-salted fries, and slid into a vinyl-upholstered booth. Sinking my teeth into the soft sesame seed bun and the juicy cheeseburger topped with my selection of everything but pickles gave me a feeling of pure satisfaction. Andy makes a great burger! I noticed a lot of locals here, which is always a sign that there's a good thing going. The hotel certainly has put a human face on its well-oiled machine, and what an open and friendly one it is at that!

I urge you to adopt the same spirit of discovery and adventure when it comes to exploring the city in general. Wandering through the many neighborhoods of New York City, I take a sort of scouting approach, like I sometimes do on an unfamiliar golf course. Instead of using motorized transportation to travel from one point to the next, I make the journey itself my destination. Take the time to walk. By slowing your pace in the fast city, you'll find a lot of interesting nooks, approachable people, and the ability to indulge your whims. You will notice things that would have otherwise passed by in a blur. After a full afternoon and evening, I headed back to my hotel, The Ritz-Carlton New York in Battery Park. The AAA 5-Diamond hotel has a beautiful location next to the water and attractive Battery Park. I especially like this location, as it is a short walk from the hotel to many points of interest, including the ferries for Ellis Island and the Statue of Liberty, which are located just across the street. I recommend choosing a room at the Ritz-Carlton with a harbor view. Telescopes in each of these rooms make for great gazing at Liberty.

New York's subway system is clean, safe, and easy. It also makes a great option for navigating around the city. The subway is even an option to access Van Cortlandt Park Golf Course in the Bronx. Take the

his clubs close by, as people were known to jump out of the bushes and steal clubs, balls, and other personal belongings! Never did he waver, though, from playing this great course in the Bronx. Even if some of the negative conditions may have been exaggerated, Van Cortlandt Park did profit greatly by an extensive renovation project, initiated by another New Yorker and avid golfer, Mayor Rudolph Giuliani, in 2001.

Like New York's subways, the course today is clean and safe. The effects of the 2001 improvement program are readily noticeable. I marveled at the pristinely manicured fairways and greens on every hole. The two reservoirs that have been added into course play are attractive and challenging, and they make self-irrigation possible. This increased ability to

I especially like this location, as it is a short walk from the hotel to many points of interest, including the ferries for Ellis Island...

Number 1 or 9. Of course, one can also drive there. Located right off the Major Deegan Expressway at Van Cortlandt Park South and Bailey Avenue, the golf course is only about a five-minute drive from famed Yankee Stadium. Some of baseball's greatest players also enjoyed golf at Van Cortlandt Park. Babe Ruth, Jackie Robinson, and Willie Mayes played here, as did Joe Louis and even the Three Stooges, who preferred this course above all others. There's a lot of folklore surrounding Van Cortlandt. While I was waiting for my tee time, I passed the time chatting with a guy who lives and works in Manhattan and who has played the course for many years.

Fifteen years ago, he explained, he had to navigate play around rusted-out cars parked around the course. He also remembers the need to play each hole with

maintain the course to the highest of standards is also an environment-conscious approach to grounds-keeping, and there wasn't a rusted car within sight! I complimented course superintendent Kevin Hoban on the course's great condition. He modestly accepted my praise, but was quick to give credit to his crew and the course's wise policies.

Van Cortlandt is open for year-round play; however, frost delays are imposed to save the grass, and a much more extensive cart path system has been laid out to keep golf carts from damaging the turf. There's a lot of new technology at work that helps keep the course in shape, but the historic grounds and original dark-wood locker rooms, dating back to 1902, preserve the link to the past. There is a wall plaque outside the club-house that gives a broad history of Van Cortlandt.

It lists Thomas Bendelow as the course's designer. Although Bendelow went on to design some 400 other golf courses, he remained at Van Cortlandt to manage the course and made golf history here by inventing the "starting time." Waiting for my "starting time," it was clear why the current popularity enjoyed by Van Cortlandt is nothing new.

The crisp morning air and clear blue sky lent the day its autumn feel. The foliage along the heavily wooded fairways was showing signs of change. A lot of ducks and geese clustered on the grass and water's edge, gearing up, no doubt, for the inevitable flight south. The 6,000-yard course plays about 1,000 yards longer due to the intersections that accommodate the presence of the Major Deegan Expressway. As a result of the expressway's proximity, the course is divided into four main sectors that must be navigated back and forth. Because of these road extensions, I recommend getting a cart.

The first sector is remarkable for its lengthier and challenging holes. It includes holes 1, 2, 12, 13, and 14. As each hole is tree-lined, an accurate tee shot is vital. Hole 2 is an impressive 600-yard par 5. The 12th hole, one of the course's other par 5's, was constructed in 2002 over former marshland. Because this green is built on sand, bank grass covers the green. By contrast, older greens that were built on clay foundations feature a combination of indigenous poa grass, enhanced by creeping bent grass seed. Both hold up well to the region's colder climate. The 14th hole is perhaps one of the course's best. The 350-yard dogleg par 4 has a little brook running through the fairway. The large natural lake bordering the right side and the green can block any drive that hooks.

The second sector, holes 3, 4, 5, 6, and 7, and the third sector, holes 8, 9, 10, and 11, follow a looped format. The 7th hole, which is a 206-yard par 3, especially can keep you on your toes with its downhill approach and very sloped green that is guarded by hefty bunkers. Just as I was about to enter the final sector, the back 4, I drove my cart under the Major Deegan Overpass. This brush with the sights and smells of automobile traffic is really one of the only reminders on the entire course that you are so close to the city. The final surprise hits as you emerge into what's generally referred to as "The Hills." Holes 15, 16, 17, and 18 are severely sloped and provide striking views from their higher elevations. The 17th is an uphill par 3, while the 18th finishes with a downhill slight dogleg left. This par 4, 283-yard hole is a makeable birdie if you can avoid the fairway bunkers.

Finish a round here by relaxing for awhile on the terrace overlooking the lake. You couldn't ask for a more tranquil or beautiful setting. Van Cortlandt Park is living proof that natural resources can be found in dense urban zones. Trails leading through the course provide access to forests, wetlands, and grasslands filled with wildlife. Black walnuts fell from trees as I played. I even munched on some wild grapes that I spotted growing near the tee box on the last hole. For $36 during the week and $42 on weekends and holidays, a round of golf at Van Cortlandt feels really good on a budget and even better on your spirits.

Should inclement weather befall your plans to golf while in New York City, swing away at The Golf Club at Chelsea Pier, an indoor driving range on the city's Upper West Side. Twenty dollars will get you 118 balls. It's open from 6:30 in the morning until 11:30 at night.

Reserve a room at the Ritz-Carlton with a harbor view, and enjoy gazing at Lady Liberty with your in-room telescope.

Or you could switch gears completely and head to Kitchen Arts & Letters on Lexington Avenue. This is the United States' largest bookstore devoted solely to books and journals dealing with food and wine.

I capped off my day with dinner at Chanterelle, located in the former 19th century Mercantile Exchange Building in the TriBeCa neighborhood. Chef David Waltuck has been creating delicious and innovative food for 24 years at his formidable restaurant and shows no signs of slowing down. I sipped Champagne and began with an *amuse-bouche* of beet soup topped with creamy goat cheese, presented by the chef in a shot glass. This pleasant pairing started off what would become a seven-course gastronomic delight. I then enjoyed the chef's version of a sashimi plate, which included beautifully presented little jewels like tuna tartare, a decadent seaweed roll containing foie gras and tuna, and a spicy piece of sashimi accented with chili. For a perfect textural contrast, Chef Waltuck garnished this plate with brightly colored cubes of pickled root vegetables. Chef Waltuck's passion for Asian cuisine has undoubtedly crept into Chanterelle's menu. This New York City native deftly balances classical cooking with a contemporary palate.

Because it was early fall, I selected the butternut squash ravioli with oxtail ragout and bay leaf cream. The herbaceous notes to the cream held the bold and earthy sweetness of the squash and meaty ragout in perfect balance. The Chateau Vincent Pouilly-Fuisse also paired well with my entrée, striped bass with red butter and fresh sage.

Chef Waltuck's menu features many foods and wines indigenous to the United States, including a wide array of artisanal cheeses. The friendly and knowledgeable cheese specialist, Adrian Murcia, who visited my table, helped me choose among the 20, or so, cheeses offered on the cheese cart that night. I particularly enjoyed the Pleasant Hill Reserve Extra Aged from Dodgeville, Wisconsin. Two other cheeses that really stood out as extraordinary were the Kapiti Kikorangi, a blue cheese from New Zealand, and the Tomme du Bergere, a raw sheep's milk cheese from Corsica. The cheeses were so exceptional I had to ask him about his source.

Adrian told me that he purchases cheese for the restaurant at Murray's in Greenwich Village, only nine blocks from my hotel. I filed away that valuable piece of information for tomorrow's adventures, and then enjoyed the meal's final courses of a roasted Jonagold apple with brandied fig ice cream and little treasures of assorted tiny chocolates and jellied candies. I left feeling perfectly sated and confident that the next day would be filled with more discoveries. Armed as I was with Adrian's cheese shop lead, I knew that I would be off to a good start.

I began the following day by riding the subway downtown to Union Square at 14th Street. Wednesday is one of the four days each week that the square sets up the city's largest farmer's market, Greenmarket, where everything—fruit and vegetables, meat, fish, poultry and eggs, dairy products, jams and honey, maple syrup, flowers and plants—is grown and sold by farmers from the region. I grabbed a coffee and an apple turnover from one vendor and browsed the market; it provides great people-watching, as well as a fun way to shop alfresco and check out the foods in season. Vendors are generally knowledgeable and willing to share what they know with the public.

A sign at Keith's Farm stand piqued my interest. It advertised its rocambole garlic as the best garlic in the world. It's an interesting variety that is planted in fall and harvested the following summer. Another booth, from Eckerton Hill Farm, must have had over two dozen varieties of peppers for sale. One, the tiny yellow wild Brazil pepper, was the size of my fingernail. Owner Tim Stark cautioned that this diminutive pepper had an extremely high heat factor.

I continued walking into Greenwich Village, past Washington Square, until I arrived at Murray's Cheese Shop at the corner of Bleeker and Cornelia Streets. In addition to its wholesale business, Murray's runs a retail store. Liz Thorpe, the store's manager, let me sample several cheeses. I confirmed the names of the

present in this milk is directly related to the makeup of a particular area and its herbs and grasses that feed the local animals. There is indeed an art to making cheese and coaxing from a single herd's milk all of its special characteristics. Murray's is not just a treasure trove for cheese lovers; it is an artisanal operation in its own right. Top restaurants trust Murray's to provide them with the finest cheese. As Murray's ships cheese all over the country, there's a good bet that the next perfect cheese you enjoy from a restaurant's cheese cart might have come from Murray's. Now that's a good slice on a course!

I continued to uncover hidden gems. From the Village, I turned north to Chelsea, where I met Marc Buzzio and Paul Valetutti of Salumeria Biellese. I remembered their salamis from my days as a chef in

Liz explained that the high quality of the foreign cheeses was largely due to the fact that they were properly aged by affineurs.

three cheeses that I had enjoyed so much at Chanterelle. Liz explained that the high quality of the foreign cheeses was largely due to the fact that they were properly aged by affineurs, or cheese experts, before being imported and sold in the store. The goat cheeses, on the other hand, are aged at Murray's. Some are wrapped in straw, while others are washed in brine, marc, or port solutions and turned until they are deemed ready for sale.

Murray's is also proud of its selection of farmstead cheeses. Only the milk of a single farm's herd is used in these handcrafted cheeses, which are superior in flavor and texture and bear the mark of *terroir*. The same qualities that contribute to the character of a fine wine—the soil, the air, and other elements and conditions—are at play in milk. A unique flavor profile

New York. These guys are still churning out the highest quality sausages and dry-cured charcuterie. If anything, they are busier than ever. Dubbed "sausage makers to the stars," they now supply most of New York's top restaurants and many others around the country with their made-to-order products.

One step into the modest retail storefront, just down the street from Madison Square Garden at the corner of 8th Avenue and 29th Street, could instantly throw anyone off the scent. Sure, you can order a delicious sub sandwich made with all their fine salamis and other cured meats, but there's little indicating that just next door and below in their basement is a complex and nearly lost art taking place. Marc Buzzio, the founder's son, explained to me how his family's Piedmontese origins have colored so much of what they do even today.

They start with a superior product, the Berkshire hog from a certified co-op that raises its animals both antibiotic and hormone-free and allows them to run and graze freely. The meat from this breed is dark, with prime marbling, and produces a more tender and flavorful product. Marc was so proud of this that he literally ripped open one of the boxes of pork bellies he had just received to show me. They reject the use of chemicals for their products, or shortcuts like artificial colors and flavors. Rather, the Old World methods of using combinations of wine, spices, natural casings, and hand tying the products before their final fermentation in a lengthy dry-curing stage preserve more than a variety of mouth-watering meats; they preserve a nearly lost art.

Marc invited me downstairs to his basement operation, where I took a peek at the dry-curing room. Interestingly enough, the temperature is set at 55 degrees, the same temperature as a wine cellar. He showed me a few products made special order that were earmarked for top New York restaurants. As custom orders rotate with demand, ask what special products are currently available to the retail customer. For another opportunity to savor a variety of their amazing meat products, dine at their adjacent restaurant, Biricchino.

I sat down with Marc and Paul in their neighborhood joint. He explained that its name is actually Piedmontese slang for "nasty little brat," a name Marc's father affectionately called him in his younger days. Marc poured me a glass of chianti and brought some

ITS NAME IS ACTUALLY PIEDMONTESE SLANG FOR "NASTY LITTLE BRAT."

extra-virgin olive oil and freshly baked country bread to the table. We proceeded to sample from a range of their currently available products. Thin slices of prosciutto Biellese were buttery in texture, with a hint of nuttiness to the palate. The outstanding coppa showed the beautiful marbling of the Berkshire hog, while the company's roots showed in the saucisson rosette, a perfect rendition of the lyonnaise-style salami from France; the spicy saucisson sec basquese; and the braesaola, an air-dried beef originally from Italy. We enjoyed a little salad of crisp lettuce and teardrop tomatoes, which accompanied a platter of mixed sausages. These included their sun-dried tomato and basil veal sausage, a variety of chicken sausages, and a spicy chorizo.

Throughout this incredible tour of sausage and charcuterie, we talked about the food trade, offering perspectives from our various areas of expertise. Once I confessed to being an avid but very average golfer, Paul volunteered that he, too, was a hack. The demands of his busy business don't allow for a lot of golf, but I knew he valued an opportunity to get out and play and did manage to sneak out now and again when he dropped a suggestion my way to help ensure a tee time at Van Cortlandt. Paul says an early morning call at 6:59 and 30 seconds made a week in advance of your desired tee time will do the trick!

My brief but satisfying golf and dining adventure was coming to a close, so I thought it apt to finish this round with a trek to Jacques Torres Chocolate in Brooklyn. Torres' factory and shop is located off the beaten path at 66 Water Street, between Dock and Main Streets. His chocolate factory is housed in a converted 120-year-old warehouse and sits on a charming cobblestone street. Big picture windows separate the retail store from the factory, giving customers great glimpses into Torres' world of chocolate creation.

All his chocolates and fillings are made from scratch. Not surprisingly, Jacques uses only fresh ingredients and no preservatives, artificial colors, or additives. He works from a grandma mentality, using copper pots and wooden spoons, and executes many techniques by hand. Coupling his talents with the latest in technology, Jacques Torres' level of expertise in chocolate making is akin to what Tiger Woods swinging away on his set of Nike clubs is to the world of golf.

Though he does not use preservatives, Torres' chocolate remains fresh through the use of a special machine that removes air from the ganache fillings. Torres borrowed this technique from the skin care industry, of all places, and cleverly applies it to chocolate making. The result is an extremely smooth and dense chocolate with intensified flavors that fill the mouth. I can personally recommend the fresh-squeezed lemon encased in dark chocolate, the creamy caramel, and the almondine, recognizable by the chocolate maker's logo etched in edible gold foil on top.

Sit at one of the store's marble tables or at the bar and indulge in a pastry made on the premises and a signature wicked hot chocolate made with chipotle chiles. This viscous liquid chocolate treat will surely heat you up. Torres is among the finest chocolate makers in the United States, but despite this, he doesn't take it all too seriously. There's an element of Willy Wonka at work here, and there's a large photograph hanging in the store of the famous chocolate factory scene from the memorable episode of I Love Lucy. His one kilo chocolate bar is called "The Big Daddy," the package describing it as a Hunka-Hunka Burnin' Love. It is clear from visiting his store and sampling his amazing chocolates that Jacques Torres is not simply creating a delicious product, he is having a great time in the process. I know the feeling. I hope you will follow my suggestions and explore some of my favorite golf and culinary destinations. With this same sense of adventure, seek out a few of your own.

Like a string of pearls, each hidden gem's discovery in New York City reveals a thriving artisanal food scene. For me, a day's adventure of building upon one after another is the gastronomic equivalent of a great round of 18. The beauty of New York City lies in its natural and man-made resources and in its ability to amass a wide variety of top quality local and international goods and make them available to consumers. New York City remains at the forefront of gastronomy because so many purveyors and restaurateurs recognize the value of not cutting any corners. From the farmer's market and the modest hamburger joint tucked away in its posh Midtown hotel lobby to the finest restaurants and their individual suppliers, you, too, can access all these treasures by assuming the spirit of adventure. Seek out the best New York City has to offer. I guarantee you will learn a lot, meet some very interesting people, and savor every bite of every moment. Great publicly accessible golf is at your fingertips as well. Whether you live in the New York City metropolitan area or are a visitor, like myself, I hope you will visit the Bronx to play Van Cortlandt Park and feel the spirit of rejuvenation that the course can work on its patrons. This golfing treasure is worth finding.

CRISPY BACON-WRAPPED PEAR WITH FRISÉE SALAD

RATING: Par for the Course on a Par 3; Average to High Greens Fees

SERVES: 4

Inspired by my culinary adventure through New York City, from the Greenmarket to Murray's Cheese Shop and Salumeria Biellese, this starter course features a product from each purveyor.

2 cups sweet wine with honeyed
  notes, such as Bonnezeaux from
  the Loire Valley
juice of 1 lemon
1 tablespoon star anise
1 teaspoon black peppercorns
4 small Forelle pears, peeled
8 to 12 ounces dry goat cheese
8 slices uncooked bacon
4 small heads frisée
4 small handfuls of arugula or
  spinach leaves
Balsamic Vinaigrette (page 176)

Combine the wine, lemon juice, star anise and peppercorns in a saucepan and bring to a boil. Place the whole pears in the liquid, making sure the liquid covers them completely. Cook over medium heat for 10 minutes until poached.

Remove the pears from the poaching liquid and let stand until cool enough to handle. Cut the pears into halves. Remove the cores with a melon ball scoop and stuff with the goat cheese. Wrap each pear half with 2 slices of bacon.

Preheat the oven to 350 degrees. Arrange the pears in a baking pan and bake for 10 to 25 minute or until the bacon is crisp, depending on the thickness of the bacon. Drain on paper towels.

Combine the frisée and arugula with the Balsamic Vinaigrette in a bowl and toss to coat well. Spoon onto serving plates. Add a warm pear to each plate.

TIP: You can poach the pears a day in advance for this dish.

SALMON WITH GRAPES IN VINEGAR

RATING: A Short Par 3; Average Greens Fees

SERVES: 4

The natural richness of the Atlantic salmon and its accompanying sweet peppery glaze is balanced by the tartness of the vinegar-soaked grapes. It's an elegant dish, but easy and quick enough to make mid-week.

3/4 cup honey or brown sugar
1 cup red wine vinegar
1/2 cup water or Vegetable Stock (page 181)
1/2 teaspoon black peppercorns
1 pound fresh seedless grapes
1/4 cup (1/2 stick) butter, sliced
salt and freshly ground pepper to taste
1 tablespoon olive oil
4 salmon fillets with skin
leaves of 4 sprigs fresh tarragon

Combine the honey, vinegar, water and peppercorns in a saucepan. Bring to a boil and reduce the heat to medium. Cook for 10 minutes. Add the grapes and cook for 10 minutes longer.

Preheat the oven to 375 degrees. Remove the grapes to a roasting pan with a slotted spoon, reserving the cooking liquid in the saucepan. Cook the reserved liquid until reduced to a syrup. Whisk in the butter. Season with salt and pepper to taste and keep warm.

Heat the olive oil in a nonstick sauté pan. Season the salmon with salt and pepper and place skin side down in the sauté pan. Cover with the tarragon leaves. Cook over medium heat for 3 to 4 minutes.

Remove the salmon to the roasting pan and arrange it skin side up over the grapes. Roast for 3 to 5 minutes or until cooked through. Remove the salmon and grapes to serving plates and spoon the honey vinegar sauce over the top.

TIP: To ensure even cooking of the salmon, be sure that the fillets are uniform in size. I recommend long, thick fillets from the meatiest part of the fish.

FRESH PASTA WITH WHITE TRUFFLE

RATING: Par for the Course on a Par 4; High Greens Fees

SERVES: 4

The United States has vast culinary resources. Take the domestic white truffle, for example. The American variety is full-bodied in flavor and aroma, and makes a fine alternative to its European counterpart.

1 recipe Fresh Pasta (page 184)
1 white truffle
2 tablespoons chopped parsley
2 to 4 tablespoons extra-virgin olive oil

Spoon the drained pasta onto serving plates. Shave the truffle over the pasta. Sprinkle with the parsley and drizzle with the olive oil.

TIP: To infuse olive oil with the flavor of white truffle, soak a small piece of the truffle in the olive oil while you prepare the pasta.

SHORT RIBS WITH SEVEN-SPICE WINE SAUCE

RATING: A Long Par 5; Average Greens Fees

SERVES: 4 to 6

This is a good dish to make the day before you serve it; the flavor of the meat will improve, and your time will be more manageable. This hearty comfort food can be served family-style or bistro-style over a generous helping of creamy mashed potatoes; your guests will no doubt help themselves to seconds!

3 tablespoons olive oil
6 pounds bone-in short ribs, trimmed
salt and freshly ground pepper to taste
1 large carrot, finely chopped
1 rib celery, finely chopped
1 small onion or 4 shallots, finely chopped
6 unpeeled garlic cloves
6 tablespoons mixed cardamom, coriander seeds,
    fennel seeds, cumin, star anise, black peppercorns
    and white peppercorns
1 bay leaf
2 tablespoons flour
1¹/₂ bottles of wine, such as cabernet sauvignon or merlot
1 tablespoon sugar
3 quarts Veal Stock (page 180) or beef stock
1 teaspoon butter
2 tablespoons chopped parsley, for garnish

Preheat the oven to 350 degrees. Preheat the olive oil in a large casserole. Season the ribs with salt and pepper. Sear the ribs in the olive oil until brown on all sides. Remove the ribs to a plate.

Add the carrot, celery, onion, garlic, spice mixture and bay leaf. Cook for 3 to 4 minutes or until the vegetable and spice flavors are released.

Return the ribs to the casserole and sprinkle with the flour. Pour the wine over the ribs. Cook on the stovetop until the wine has been reduced by ¹/₂. Sprinkle with the sugar and add the Veal Stock.

Roast in the oven for about 2 hours, basting every 20 minutes and checking for tenderness. Strain the cooking juices into a 3-quart saucepan, pressing out as much liquid as possible. Keep the ribs warm.

Bring the cooking juices to a boil. Check and adjust the seasoning. Cook for 15 to 20 minutes if necessary to reduce the sauce to the desired consistency. Remove from the heat and whisk in the butter to balance the spice flavor and give the sauce a nice sheen.

Place the ribs in a serving dish and spoon the sauce over the top. Garnish with chopped parsley.

TIP: Take the time to brown the ribs properly before baking; it will improve the flavor.

BLONDE BROWNIES

RATING: Par for the Course on a Par 3; Low Greens Fees

MAKES: About 30

My dining adventure in New York City started with brownies at the Burger Joint and ends with a playful homage to Jacques Torres, "Mr. Chocolate" himself. The attractive blonde crust on these treats yields to a rich, chewy center. The result is an easy, surprising twist to the typical brownie. I guarantee that they will not disappoint the chocolate lover.

1 cup (2 sticks) butter, softened
2 1/4 cups sugar
1 1/4 cups flour
4 eggs
1/2 cup toasted chopped almonds
4 ounces semisweet chocolate, chopped, or
  chocolate disks

Preheat the oven to 350 degrees. Cream the butter and sugar with a paddle attachment in a mixing bowl.

Add the flour and then beat in the eggs 1 at a time. Fold in the chopped almonds and chocolate. Spread in a 9×13-inch baking pan. Bake for 45 minutes or until golden brown.

"Big Apple" Tart

RATING: A Long Par 4; Average Greens Fees

SERVES: 8

You can't think New York without thinking "The Big Apple," so a chapter on New York must include an apple recipe. This tart features the apple in not one, but two, forms. Top a thick apple compote with baked apple slices for a big apple taste!

1 recipe Pâte Sucrée (page 187)
1 1/2 cups apple compote or
    thickened cinnamon applesauce
4 to 6 Granny Smith apples, peeled,
    cored and sliced 1/8 inch thick
1/2 cup sugar

Preheat the oven to 350 degrees. Shape the Pâte Sucrée into a ball and roll it evenly into a circle 1/4 inch thick on a work surface dusted with flour. Roll the dough around the rolling pin and transfer to an 11-inch tart pan. Press the dough lightly against the edge and cut off the excess dough by rolling the pin over the pan.

Spread the apple compote evenly over the tart, leaving 3/4 inch space for the apple slices. Arrange the apples slices over the compote in 2 layers of overlapping circles, beginning at the outer edge and working toward the center; fill in any spaces with small apple pieces. Sprinkle evenly with the sugar. Bake for about 1 1/2 hours or until golden brown.

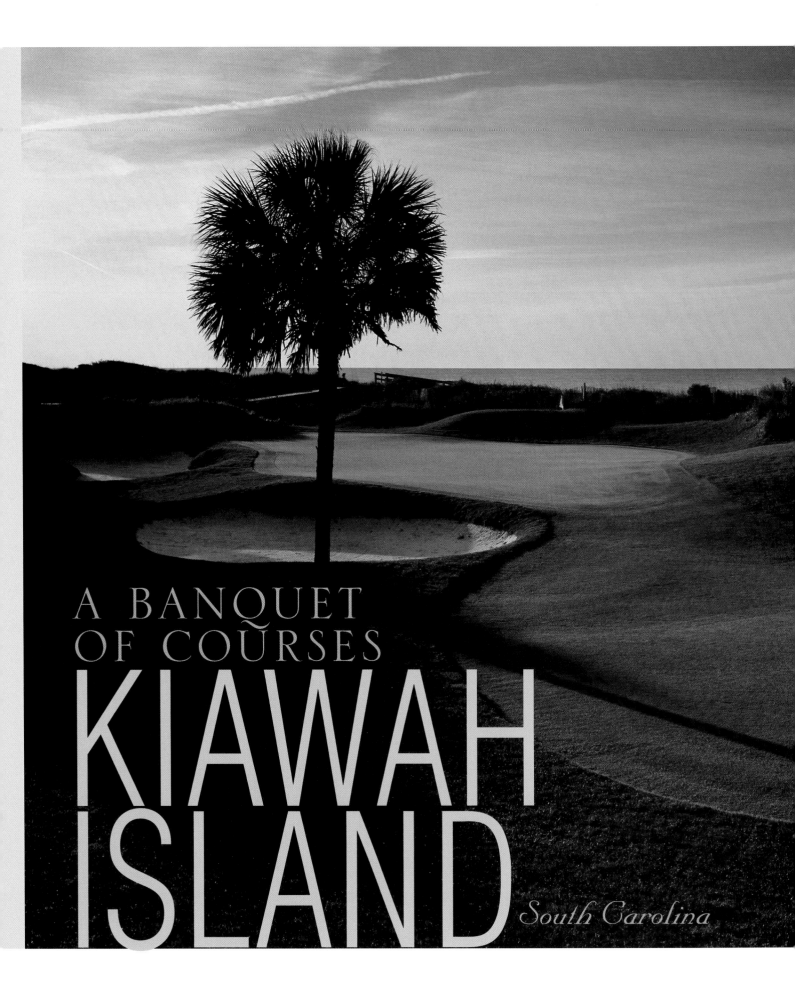

A BANQUET
OF COURSES
KIAWAH
ISLAND

South Carolina

The Ocean Course, site of the 1991 Ryder Cup Matches, was named the most difficult course in North America by Golf Digest. Severe winds off the ocean affect both the landscape and the golfing.

I have wanted to come to Kiawah Island, South Carolina, ever since I watched the televised 1991 Ryder Cup Matches played on the island's Ocean Course. The dramatic moment on which the whole tournament came to rest, on the last day and last hole of play, when Bernhard Langer missed his putt, is still a hot topic in golf circles. The competition and the devastatingly difficult seaside links course, so beautiful in its rawness, is etched in my mind.

I arrived midday at Charleston's airport and drove the 21 miles to Kiawah Island. Just before arriving, I spotted an open market called Rosebank Farms on neighboring Johns Island. As it was lunchtime, my stomach, as well as my curiosity, prompted the quick detour. The moment I walked into the shaded market, a chicken crossed my path. Their kind of direct advertising made it clear that guinea eggs for sale here are undoubtedly laid by free-range chickens! Besides the fresh fish, shrimp, and crab meat for sale in coolers, I found plenty of local specialties to sample on the premises or to take with me to munch on in the car.

Bottles of soda pop on ice, perfect vine-and tree-ripened fruits and vegetables, dry and canned goods all tempted me. I grazed on a few delectable boiled shrimp that sat on ice, waiting for a hungry customer to try. Then, I spotted the huge cauldron full of boiled peanuts. There was a slow cooker near it, with a couple of guys hunched over it, gobbling up a handful of the warm, salty snack. They warned me that I might get thirsty from the peanuts, as they served me up a handful and helped themselves to another. The shells were addictive, juicy and salty, and the peanuts inside were surprisingly soft and sweet. It was a little like eating peanut butter, but without the pitfalls: no getting tongue-tied with a sticky palate. On the contrary, my fellow peanut eaters and I fell into easy conversation.

Sanctuary at East Beach Village, a brand-new, elegant, 255-room, oceanfront hotel. Among the dining options that guests can choose from here are fireside afternoon tea while looking out to the Atlantic; terraced oceanfront dining; a more intimate setting in the private wine room; or a casual terraced restaurant that serves breakfast, lunch, and dinner. If golf is your passion then you will love the ten rooms available over the clubhouse, on the Ocean Course's 18th hole. The exclusive course-side locale, with unparalleled views of the Atlantic Ocean, is expected to open in 2005.

Hitting the area golf courses is one fine way to experience the island's natural diversity. A barrier island, Kiawah is comprised of five distinct habitats,

These would make great gifts if I could resist.

It was hard to leave this unexpected friendly communal repast, but I was starting to feel guilty about the quantity of peanuts I was consuming "on the house." I purchased a hot to-go bag of the peanuts, a bottle of soda, some grapes, and a few jars of pickled okra and dilled green beans. These would make nice gifts if I could resist the temptation to eat them over the course of my visit here.

A short time later, I arrived on the island. There is a variety of lodging options when you come to Kiawah. One-to six-bedroom rental villas are available, which can be especially convenient for families who prefer to cook some of their own meals. One hotel choice is the Kiawah Island Inn, located at West Beach Village. This pedestrian-friendly facility has 150 rooms, a pool, a tennis complex, and shops nearby. There is also The

which make up the Maritime Strand. During your explorations on Kiawah, you will come across tidal creeks, salt marshes, salt flats, thickets, maritime forests, and the spectacular ocean dunes. Another great way to get to know the island is to select from the many options available to the resort's guests at the Heron Park Nature Center in the East Beach Village enclave. There are interesting exhibits at the center and a host of activities available. Kayaking and canoeing can take you through rivers, marshes, and the Atlantic Ocean, while a variety of nature walks offers an opportunity to view alligators, birds, botany, and the loggerhead sea turtles.

The island's inhabitants are extremely sensitive to the island's wildlife. For example, outdoor lights are not permitted during loggerhead sea turtle nesting season. This endangered species lay its eggs in the moonlit marshes, so the ban on artificial lights prevents the turtles from mistakenly laying precious eggs in unsafe areas. The low-light conditions can make for tricky night driving; I think I'll save the cool, windy roads for a daytime motorcycle ride!

When I heard about seining at the nature center, I thought it sounded like a unique way to learn more about the animals that live in the ocean. Seining takes place right on the beach at low tide. I met with Elizabeth, one of the resort's naturalists, who was waiting for me with the seining equipment. The large net had weights on one side so that the net would drag over the ocean floor. Floats lined the other side, allowing the net to skim the water's surface. Each of us grabbed a pole on either side of the large net and waded into the warm water until it was up to our knees. The trick to seining is to keep your pole at an angle. This maintains a drag on the net's low side. We walked parallel to the beach; then Elizabeth circled around with her side, and we pulled our catch onto the beach.

There were a lot of anchovies. We joked that I could use them for a pizza or to top a niçoise salad! We also pulled out one small whiting and some tiny pompano. This was my idea of a great classroom setting to learn about our catch. Even on the tiniest fish we were able to observe countershading, a phenomenon that provides fish with a natural protection against predators. The dark side on top of fish protects against birds of prey, while the light underside camouflages them from larger fish. These fish had nothing to fear from us. Elizabeth stored them in a small case filled with seawater until we were finished with our session. Then, we released the catch back into the ocean.

While our catch did not yield any sizable fish, the seining was still fun. Each time, you're likely to drag in something of interest. Elizabeth said someone pulled up a small shark once. Their largest fish caught to date was a 3-foot bluefish. It's also possible to pull up shrimp, crab, and flounder. Since my seining did not provide an opportunity to taste any of the ocean's bounty, I headed for Mingo Point, where I was sure to enjoy a unique and delicious Carolina tradition—an oyster roast.

Surrounded by palm trees, with the Atlantic Ocean in view, Mingo Point is set on the banks of the Kiawah River. The Native American Kiawahs who lived in this region were a peaceful group of fishermen. The oldest known account of an oyster roast dates back to 1566, when these native peoples served roasted oysters to Spanish explorers near Charleston. M. C. was tonight's host of the oyster roast. His method of roasting oysters was passed down from his father. Dressed in denim overalls and a straw hat, M. C., whose name was befitting for such a master of ceremony, readied the barbecue by splitting wood and starting the fire. He cleaned the large, flat metal cooking surface with fresh water, creating a lot of steam—a hot surface, indeed, for cooking the oysters.

> THE NATIVE AMERICAN KIAWAHS WHO LIVED IN THIS REGION WERE A PEACEFUL GROUP OF FISHERMEN.

M. C. recommends using large oysters. After placing them on the hot metal, he covers the oysters with burlap saturated in fresh water. M. C. explained that the first phase of cooking is steaming. The second phase, smoke roasting, enhances the oyster's sweet and salty flavor. No added seasonings are necessary. After just a few minutes of cooking, M. C. pointed out the telltale sign of doneness—the popping noise. At this stage, the oysters are cooked to a medium doneness, and the popping sound indicates the presence of flavorful juices. Cooking too long could produce a tough, dry oyster.

M. C. shoveled the perfectly cooked oysters onto a weather-beaten wooden table stacked with pewter plates and bowls full of traditional accompaniments, like lemon wedges, Tabasco sauce, cocktail sauce, saltine crackers, and, of course, the ubiquitous packages of Handi Wipes. Because they are cooked, the oysters are very easy to pry open. M. C. suggests using an oyster knife to cut the back end of the oyster's hinge. I doctored mine up with lemon juice and a dab of cocktail sauce to mingle with the oyster's natural juices. What a great way to end my first day of getting to know Kiawah! You, too, will love

On Kiawah Island, five glorious golf courses are laid out like a banquet for the golf lover.

eating oysters while watching the sun set over the Kiawah River. It's no wonder that the oyster roast is the resort's most popular activity.

The following morning, I headed right back to the same area to tee off at Cougar Point. Of the five courses located on Kiawah Island—Oak Point, designed by Clyde Johnston, Osprey Point, designed by Tom Fazio, Jack Nicklaus' Turtle Point, and the Ocean Course, designed by Pete Dye—it's Cougar Point that really connects the golfer to the Low Country. The early morning shadows that danced against the softly sloping fairways and the dramatic sweeping vistas

along the Kiawah River and surrounding salt marshes are typical Low-Country highlights, which characterize this very natural course.

Cougar Point ranks right up there with the other top courses on the island. Gary Player's 1996 course redesign earned 4 1/2 stars in *Fodor's/Golf Digest Places to Play* ratings book. Cougar Point starts out with a short par 4. This hole, as well as the other short par 4's, numbers 7, 8, 16, and 17, are target-style holes and call for accuracy. Holes 4, 5, 10, 13, and 18 are long par 4's with wide fairways to help navigate the best angles for tricky pin placement. The course plays fair.

I appreciated the generously sized greens on the par 5's, which allowed for the gutsy long shot without taking an undue risk that the ball would roll right off the green.

As spectacular views go, it doesn't get much better than from holes 6 and 17. At the 6th hole, it was high tide, so the marshes were mostly covered by water. The Kiawah River estuary bordered right, providing a signature Low Country panorama. At 158 yards, this challenging par 3 is longer than it appears. Club selection was tricky for me.

The beautiful views and playing options increased tremendously at the 17th. With water playing down the entire right side and a large tree strategically placed just before a large bunker at the fairway's midpoint, there are plenty of obstacles to navigate on this makeable birdie par 4. My first ball hit the water, and though I already had a two-shot penalty, I decided to continue playing aggressively. I went for it! My second attempt sailed over the water right to the pin, and I sank the gimme for par. Sometimes, recoveries are just as exciting as birdies.

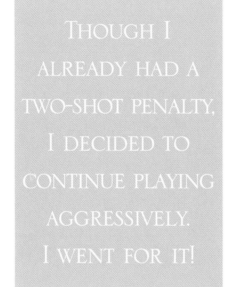

THOUGH I ALREADY HAD A TWO-SHOT PENALTY, I DECIDED TO CONTINUE PLAYING AGGRESSIVELY. I WENT FOR IT!

The rush of adrenaline sparked my hunger. I wanted to learn more about Low-Country cuisine, while sampling it, of course. Also, I had to find out the whole story on how Kiawah Island Golf Resort managed to secure Vijay Singh as its food and beverage director! I love it when I find a blurring of the boundaries between the worlds of golf and cooking, and I'm not a shy guy. A little probing back at the inn cleared up my misconception. While Mr. Singh is not the noted professional golfer, it does seem fitting that at a world-class golf resort, even a staff member bears the name of one of golf's elite.

So much for meeting Mr. Singh. I did have the good fortune of meeting Matthew Neissner, the executive chef at the inn's Atlantic Room, who was most willing to provide me with a culinary primer. His spread paired smoked meats and seafood with stone-ground white grits cooked in milk and butter, succotash, and other local produce such as corn, collards, okra, tomatoes, and butter beans. He explained that Low-Country food blends the culinary influences of the French, English, Spanish, and African cultures that merged with the Native Americans' customs in the thriving port town of Charleston in the seventeenth century.

Some examples of this melding of culinary traditions can be found in she-crab soup; it starts with a Scottish porridge base to which is added local blue crab that is further enhanced by Spanish sherry. Succotash is a Narraganset word meaning "boiled whole kernels of corn." The familiar Southern dish prepared at the resort also contained lima beans and red and green bell peppers, all of which thrive in the Low Country. Fertile land and a temperate climate make prime farmland and perfect conditions for the popular pasttime of backyard vegetable gardening. Even the friendly semiretired gentleman who shuttled me to and from Charleston later that evening tends to a thriving garden of squash, melons, tomatoes, and beans.

As he walked me through the various dishes, Chef Neissner readied a large stockpot for a seafood boil. He boiled white wine and water and flavored it with bay leaves, pickled garlic, jalapeño chiles, crab boil seasoning, and sea salt. He then added parboiled potatoes, ears of corn, chunks of zucchini, smoked sausage, wild-river clams, blue crabs, and local shrimp. While we discussed Low-Country cuisine, incredible smells began wafting out of the pot. Shortly thereafter, the chef poured the entire pot's contents directly onto a banquet table. With this pièce de résistance, he demonstrated the essence of Low-Country cuisine: Not only is the meal both something purely American and greater than the sum of its divergent parts, it's also the means by which it is customarily consumed. A seafood boil, like so much of the cooking from these parts, is all about bounty and is best eaten with a large group, an extended family, or a party with lots of friends. Low-Country food is communal and celebratory. It is complex in its profile of flavors and textures and in its origins.

In addition to offering superb traditional Low-Country cooking, the area continues to be at the forefront of innovative Low-Country cuisine. It is worthwhile to include a visit to Charleston. The resort offers a convenient shuttle service to the city. The historic city is full of charming examples of colonial, antebellum, and Victorian architecture. Its small scale allows for easy strolling. When you are ready to take a break, The Library on Vendue Range makes a great stop for a picturesque setting. Enjoy a cocktail and the view of the harbor while you relax at its rooftop bar. Then, continue on into Charleston's historic French Quarter to 82 Queen on Queen Street. The restaurant has a garden courtyard that instantly transports you to an earlier era as you dine on deliciously prepared authentic Low-Country dishes.

During the rest of my stay on Kiawah Island, I played two more courses. They couldn't have been more different in terrain or in personality. Osprey Point is a park-side course with four large natural lakes and dense forests of century-old live oaks, magnolia and pine trees, and palmetto palms. Leaning trees and some gaps are remaining signs of Hurricane Hugo which swept the island in 1989. These signs of nature's fury are tempered by the fairness of the course itself. Known for his friendly golf course design, Tom Fazio's Osprey Point is a course to which I feel that I relate well and that I can attack. When the afternoon Kiawah sea breezes picked up and became difficult to contend with, I switched to more of a bump-and-run ground game. This course is forgiving and offers options for the golfer when the winds prove too challenging.

At The Ocean Course, by contrast, there is nowhere to hide. Wind is a huge factor and one of the course's most distinctive features. On the day that I played, I commented on how windy it was to my golfing companion, Director of Golf Roger Warren, and he told me it was pretty calm by Kiawah standards! The dramatic effects of the wind are everywhere. Sand dunes are constantly eroding and changing contour. Consequently, most of the sand on The Ocean Course is treated as waste bunker. Players are permitted to ground their clubs, but I took little comfort in this unique exception that allowed me to take practice swings when I found myself faced with a 20-foot sand headwall or an expanse of 50 yards of sand with which to reckon. The wind also makes dramatic effects on the way the trees and bushes grow. Unlike the calm and stately magnolias and live oaks on the Osprey Point course, "wind pruning" on The Ocean Course causes the trees to look as if they are tossing a head of hair back as a strong wind blows against its face.

From the back tees, The Ocean Course has a 79.6 *Course Rating*, one of the highest in the world. No wonder *Golf Digest* named it the most difficult resort course in North America. It's a par 72, and the course record from the gold tee is a 72. On the flip side, Kiawah Island Resorts has implemented a walking caddie program, which lessens the intimidation factor. Knowledgeable caddies like Terry Seay and Danny Gourley understand the wind and particularities of the course and offer insightful suggestions to best play your game. Though the resort encourages players to walk, forecaddies are available to non-walking guests as well. Terry and Danny also provided a lot of local color and were quick to point out the alligators when they became visible. Probably the only thing that Osprey Point and The Ocean Course have in common, other than both being golf courses, is that both are very fair.

Pete Dye may have designed one of the most challenging golf courses ever to exist, but his design utilizes severities found in nature; he does not resort to cheap tricks. Very few blind spots exist on the seaside links course. There are as many as six tee boxes on some holes, which allow players to adjust their shots depending on whether they are hitting with or into the ever-changing wind. Dye took into account that players will hit both long and short approach shots, depending on weather conditions. He addressed the need for flexible play by designing large greens and planting them with roll-resistant grass.

As I played each hole, I envisioned highlights from the 1991 Ryder Cup, which took place on this course. I took comfort that Calcavecchio drove a ball into the water at the 17th, as did O'Meara twice. I felt inspired by memories of O'Meara hitting a five-foot putt for eagle and the four straight birdies that Couples and Floyd made during the event's 4-Ball competition. For all the hype that the Ryder Cup has received as a "war by the shore," I like to remember it for the perspective it gives to sports and sportsmanship. Hale Irwin's statement following the United States' victory in 1991 speaks to the transcendent powers of golf. He said that it was wonderful to feel so close to the people he was playing against. Like Hale Irwin, I play golf for the love of game, for the sense of comradeship, and to connect with the land. Playing The Ocean Course might have felt like a battle every step of the way in the Ryder Cup competition, as it certainly did to me when I recently encountered it, but, like Hale Irwin, I did not leave war-torn. On the contrary, I left that course feeling like I had tussled with an old friend. I felt exuberant that I finally had the chance to come to Kiawah Island, to explore a fascination more than ten years in the making, and play the famed Ocean Course.

Like the Low-Country cuisine, highlighted by its oyster roasts and seafood boils, golf here at Kiawah Island is best described along the lines of a banquet. It's all laid out for the golf lover to enjoy. All five glorious courses on the island offer a specific feature of the island's many highlights. Come to Kiawah Island for the feast. I guarantee that you will want to take a second and a third helping!

GOUGÈRES

RATING: Par for the Course on a Par 4; Average Greens Fees

MAKES: about 3 dozen hors d'oeuvre pieces

Start out any feast with a gougère. These bite-size delights are wonderful for a leisurely weekend breakfast or brunch. They are an elegant accompaniment to lunchtime soup and salad, and they make a perfect hot appetizer to offer to guests during the cocktail hour.

1 recipe Pâte à Choux (page 185)
3/4 cup (about) grated Gruyère cheese

Preheat the oven to 425 degrees. Follow the instructions for the Pâte à Choux, mixing the grated Gruyère cheese into the dough. Shape the dough into balls and place on a baking sheet lined with a nonstick baking mat or parchment paper.

Bake for 15 minutes. Check for browning and reduce the oven temperature to 375 degrees and bake for about 7 minutes longer or until the gougères appear dry; cooking time for the Pâte may be reduced because of the cheese.

Remove from the oven and enjoy!

TIP: The amount of grated cheese used should be 1/3 the amount of the Pâte à Choux.

BAKED CLAMS

RATING: A Short Par 3; Average Greens Fees

SERVES: 4

I took inspiration from the Mingo Point Oyster Roast for this clam dish, and when weather permits, I like to cook it in heavy-duty foil on the grill. The stovetop is a fine cooking alternative. Either way, make sure you have some crusty bread on hand to sop up the wine-laden broth.

*2 tablespoons Garlic Butter
  (page 182)
1 tomato, finely chopped
24 littleneck clams
1 cup dry white wine
freshly ground pepper to taste
salt to taste (optional)
1 tablespoon chopped parsley*

Warm the Garlic Butter in a sauté pan and add the chopped tomato. Cook over low heat for 2 to 3 minutes to sweat. Add the clams and cook for 1 minute. Stir in the wine and cover. Cook for 8 minutes.

Grind a bit of pepper on the clams and check for seasoning; it may not be necessary to add salt because the clams are naturally salty. Sprinkle with the chopped parsley and serve.

TIP: Discard any uncooked clams that are not closed. After cooking, discard any clams that have not opened. Although the rest of the dish is safe to eat, it is not recommended that you eat the unopened clams.

Seafood Boil

RATING: A Short Par 3; High Greens Fees

SERVES: 4

Chef Neissner's rendition of a seafood boil, a delicious and memorable meal, features a spicy palette of flavors; my seafood boil uses a subtler blend of spices to act as the supporting cast to the real stars of this dish, the seafood itself.

2 tablespoons olive oil
1 small onion, cut into quarters
4 potatoes, coarsely chopped
1 teaspoon coriander seeds
1 star anise
1 garlic head, cut into halves horizontally
2 ribs celery, coarsely chopped
4 scallions, coarsely chopped
8 cherry tomatoes
4 small thick pieces sea bass steaks
4 oysters
4 sea scallops
4 razor clams
2 cups hot Vegetable Stock (page 181)
salt and freshly ground pepper to taste

Heat the olive oil in a medium saucepan. Add the onion, potatoes, coriander seeds, star anise, garlic, celery, scallions and tomatoes. Sweat over low heat for 5 minutes.

Increase the heat to medium-high and add the sea bass, oysters, scallops and clams. Stir in the Vegetable Stock. Cook for 8 to 12 minutes, removing the seafood as it becomes opaque and the mollusks as they open.

Season with salt and pepper and discard the bay leaf. Serve hot with mixed greens on the side.

TIP: You can achieve the best flavor for your seafood boil if you remove the seafood before it is completely cooked and reserve it in the refrigerator while you finish cooking the remaining ingredients. Let cool for a few hours and reheat everything together just before serving.

LEMON PICKLE

RATING: A Gimme; Average Greens Fees

MAKES: About 1 cup

Pickling is second nature to me; it's a family tradition. My grandparents always pickled vegetables from their garden. The Kiawah Island region is also big on pickling foods. It's a great way to extend the garden's bounty. Among other uses, this pickle makes a zesty accompaniment to Seafood Boil (page 135).

2 medium lemons
2 tablespoons olive oil
2 teaspoons mustard seeds
4 bay leaves
1 teaspoon coriander seeds
1/4 teaspoon chili powder
1/4 cup rice wine vinegar
1/4 teaspoon lavender blossoms

Wash the lemons and cut into small pieces, discarding the seeds. Heat the olive oil in a small sauté pan. Add the mustard seeds and sauté until they begin to pop. Add the bay leaves and coriander seeds.

Reduce the heat and stir in the chili powder. Cook until the chili powder is brown. Add the vinegar and stir in the lavender and lemon.

Remove the sauté pan from the heat and allow the contents to cool. Store in a glass jar in the refrigerator for up to 1 week.

Oven-Roasted Free-Range Chicken

RATING: Par for the Course on a Par 4; Average Greens Fees

SERVES: 4

Here is my opportunity to discuss the benefits of purchasing poultry of the best quality. A chicken is only as good as its grower and processor. Look for a free-range chicken, one that receives fresh air and exercise and grazes on organic pastures like I found at Rosebank Farms on Johns Island. Not only are you getting a tastier bird, but your purchase also supports a synergistic system of total farming.

1 (3- to 4-pound) free-range chicken
1/4 cup cooking-grade olive oil
2 teaspoons dried herbes de Provence
2 tablespoons cooking-grade olive oil
2 tablespoons mixture of whole coriander seeds, black
    peppercorns, white peppercorns, fennel seeds and
    dried orange peel
salt and freshly ground pepper to taste
2 garlic heads, separated into cloves with the skins intact
1 tablespoon butter

Preheat the oven to 325 degrees. Rinse and dry the chicken inside and out. Mix 1/4 cup olive oil and the herbes de Provence in a small bowl and rub the chicken inside and out with the mixture.

Preheat a roasting pan on the stovetop and add 2 tablespoons olive oil. Sear the chicken in the oil until golden brown on all sides, ending with the back. Add the mixed spices to the cavity and season with salt and pepper.

Roast for 40 minutes. Reduce the oven temperature to 300 degrees and add the garlic cloves to the roasting pan. Place the butter in the chicken cavity and roast for 30 minutes longer or until the juices run clear; check by piercing the meaty portion of the thigh.

Place the chicken on a cutting board to rest for several minutes before carving.

TIP: Save the roasted garlic from the roasting pan; it is a delicious spread on bread.

GRITS

RATING: Par for the Course on a Par 4; Low Greens Fees

SERVES: 4

Grits, a staple of Southern cuisine, are delicious to eat anywhere and with any meal. Infusing the milk with garlic and thyme gives the grits a sophisticated flavor. Experiment with other flavorful combinations, or omit the herbal component altogether for a simpler flavor profile that can even be sweetened for children. The dish is easy to prepare, but you'll need a little "elbow grease" when whisking the grits and milk.

5 garlic cloves
7 sprigs thyme
4 cups milk
1¹/2 cups uncooked yellow or white
    cornmeal grits
1 tablespoon Garlic Butter
    (page 182)
salt and freshly ground pepper
    to taste

Tie the garlic and thyme sprigs in a cheesecloth sachet. Bring the milk to a simmer in a saucepan. Remove from the heat and add the sachet; let steep for 10 minutes and remove the sachet.

Whisk in the grits. Cook over very low heat for 15 minutes or until the milk is absorbed, whisking constantly. Stir in the Garlic Butter and season with salt and pepper.

TIP: Any leftover grits can be spread in a shallow pan, chilled, and sliced. The slices can be pan-fried or grilled and topped as for bruschetta.

A BANQUET OF COURSES KIAWAH ISLAND

BENNE WAFERS

RATING: Par for the Course on a Par 3; Low Greens Fees

MAKES: About 2 dozen

Charleston is especially known for its tiny crispy sesame benne wafers. They make a nice pairing with tea and coffee as a light finish to a Southern gastronomic feast. You can use a biscuit cutter, another Southern kitchen staple, to make the larger wafers called for in this recipe, or make them more traditional in size to yield a large batch of crunchy bite-size wafers.

> *2 cups flour*
> *¹/₂ cup sugar*
> *1 pinch of salt*
> *6 tablespoons (³/4 stick) butter*
> *¹/4 cup toasted black sesame seeds*
> *¹/4 cup toasted white sesame seeds*
> *2 egg yolks*

Preheat the oven to 350 degrees. Combine the flour, sugar and salt in a mixing bowl. Cut the butter into the dry ingredients until it has a coarse cornmeal consistency, using 2 knives in a crisscross motion. Add the sesame seeds and egg yolks; mix well. Add enough water to form a dough.

Roll the dough ¹/8 inch thick on a lightly floured surface. Cut into 4-inch rounds. Place on an ungreased baking sheet. Bake for 15 minutes or until light golden brown. Remove to a wire rack to cool.

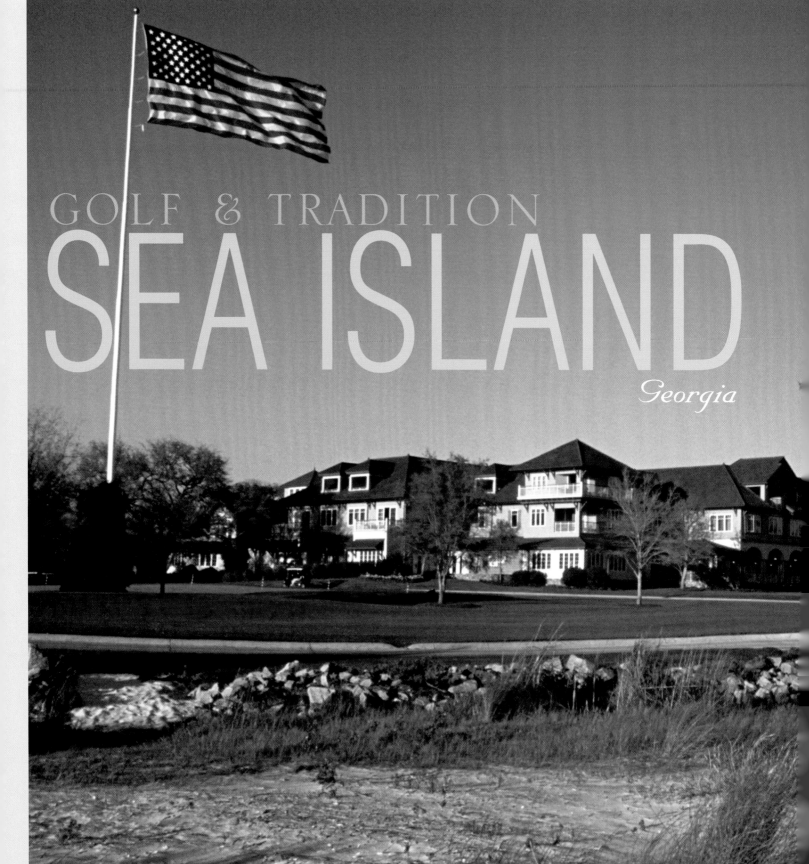

GOLF & TRADITION
SEA ISLAND
Georgia

The Lodge at Sea Island evokes the feel of a centuries-old Scottish manor. A unique sunset ritual follows through with the Scottish theme.

Sea Island cotton is what most people think of when Sea Island is mentioned.

Indeed, cotton production has been a long-standing industry on the island. Yet the island's countless other resources are the real draw for me. Their powerful links to past traditions are extremely relevant to present life on Sea Island. One feels a strong connection to the origins of golf, indigenous wildlife, and the stately grounds and buildings that comprise the Sea Island Golf Resort. Getting there is not difficult. Sea Island is located equidistant between Jacksonville, Florida, and Savannah, Georgia. In fact, the drive itself helps to set the mood for this special place.

I crossed over from the mainland to Georgia's Golden Isles via the brilliant white Sidney Lanier bridge. The striking chartreuse fields of marsh grasses and the deep blue waters of the Intracoastal Waterway jolted me with their gorgeous colors and textural contrasts. After marveling at the initial riot of color, the late-summer drive to Sea Island, Georgia, eased me into a relaxed state. The landscape reflected an atmosphere of Southern gentility and gracious formality. Tree canopies of live oaks, draped with their distinctive hanging moss, lined much of my drive. I kept thinking of how these stately trees personify a reverence for the past and its traditions.

I pulled into the porte cochere at Sea Island's original oceanfront resort hotel, The Cloister, which was designed by renowned Palm Beach architect Addison Mizner and opened in 1928. In an instant, a friendly and confident valet greeted me and pointed me toward the front desk. I walked into the Mediterranean-style hotel, at once noticing its refined, Old World feel. My room overlooked the hotel's inner courtyard and fountain. The setting was intimate, and it felt elegant yet comfortable in its small scale. I did not linger in my room for long. Dusk was fast approaching, and I did not want to miss the evening's highlight at The Lodge nearby.

was broken only by the music of a lone bagpiper, and by the striking image this solitary figure, in full regalia, cut against the natural beauty in the distance. The effect was haunting.

Immersed in this scene, I instantly felt the hushed but palpable stirrings of golf's beginnings. The obvious reverence for tradition that I was basking in at Sea Island offered me in that rare moment a link to golf's roots. There was something almost magical in that moment suspended between day and night. I felt spirited into a heritage that is so much bigger than the rushed humdrum of our everyday lives. I was truly

The striking chartreuse fields of marsh grasses and the deep blue waters of the Intracoastal Waterway jolted me with their gorgeous colors and textural contrasts.

Though just constructed in 2001, The Lodge evokes the feel of a centuries-old Scottish manor. It has a sense of timelessness, thanks to its fine appointments, mature landscaping, and unique sunset ritual. I was not really sure what to expect from the desk clerk's description of a sunset cocktail hour with bagpipes, so I admit that I was a bit skeptical about all the fuss. As I emerged onto The Lodge's back terrace, I was awestruck, and my doubts were erased as I took in the expansive view of the verdant lawn and its backdrop of a mighty delta where the Frederica River feeds into the Atlantic Ocean. The peaceful evening stillness

inspired by the evening's events and wanted to savor the mood.

I eased into one of the Adirondack chairs on the lawn and sipped an aperitif while contemplating the game of golf and my passion for it. Eventually I headed inside to the Oak Room Bar at The Lodge. Its dark-stained wood interior contributes to its casual, but clubby, atmosphere. I tried the daily special—a nicely aged steak with Roquefort mashed potatoes. A full-bodied pinot noir rounded off the meal perfectly. For dessert, I indulged in a crème brûlée, traditional perhaps, but flawlessly executed.

With the sounds of the bagpipes echoing in my ears, I retired to my room back at The Cloister for a restful night's sleep. Three stellar golf courses awaited me just on the other side of my dreams.

The sunset cocktail hour with bagpipes the night before had indeed put me into a contemplative state; with bright daylight the next morning, I laid all my evening's musings aside to literally sink my feet into the very real and tactile experiences waiting for me on the course. I chose to play the Sea Island Golf Club's Retreat Course first because it was the original course on the island. Built in 1927, the course was revamped and redesigned in 2000 by an island resident and future golf legend, Davis Love III. With ties to golf's glorious past, the Retreat Course offers the same basic routing as the original design, but the fairways are now longer and wider. Avoiding a lot of man-made obstacles, Love utilized ones that are naturally found in the area.

I was feeling really good; my swing was loose and easy, and I gained confidence from the course that I knew I would need for the Plantation and Seaside Courses. Even the missed opportunities on the tougher holes did not prevent me from feeling that breaking par on a few holes was still within reach. For instance, the 6th hole, a 300-yard par 4 had a lot of obstacles. Water lay to the front and right of the tee boxes, while sand traps littered the fairway and the green's peripheries. A short drive would leave a second shot in trouble for sure. I teed off to the middle of the fairway and landed my second shot 80 yards from the hole, onto the first cut. The day's pin placement was on the back left of the very large green. The large dip that ran through the middle of the green gave me less of a

problem than the green's slight downward slope. I misread the break and missed an opportunity to birdie but still managed par.

Despite some putting errors, I felt that I was navigating the course's demanding angles to the green pretty well and was able to play some respectable par golf. On first impression, the 18th hole, a long par 4 at 349 yards, looks like a really tough one. I needed to maximize that first shot and angle it toward the safe middle part of the fairway. I started from the left side of the tee box because of the water on my left and the out-of-bounds play to the right. I kept thinking that if I sliced this shot, I was cooked! My ball took a great roll and landed 129 yards from the hole. My second shot just missed, to the right of the green. From a slight embankment I chipped onto the green and putted in for par.

Well, my score, though respectable by my standards, wasn't going to get me any closer to rubbing shoulders on the course with golf's greats, so I headed into the Davis Love Grill, where I could at least relax in my element and view the course's driving range. I learned that the restaurant is actually named for Davis Love III's father, who joined Sea Island's golf staff in the late 1970s. While Davis Love, Jr., spent his career giving golf instruction, his young son blossomed into one of the most talented golfers on the PGA circuit. By 1985, Davis Love III became the representative for the Sea Island Golf Club on the PGA Tour. It's a pretty cool feeling to know that the Retreat Course is not simply a Davis Love III design, but that this golfing phenomenon literally grew up here learning the game and playing these courses. For me, playing this course was a little like playing in Love's backyard!

It would be a huge stretch to imagine that eating lunch at the grill is like dining in Love's kitchen, though the golf tee that held my sandwich in place rather than the typical toothpick was a nice touch. I came to learn that although the grill is named for Davis Love, Jr., the restaurant, as with all of the other restaurants at Sea Island's resort, is overseen by Executive Chef Todd Rogers. I must admit I hadn't yet met a chef who wears cowboy boots, but I can say that Chef Todd is in charge of an amazing operation. Running the gamut from tailor-made picnic baskets and daily buffets with artfully presented edible and sculpted food to steak, seafood, and large banquets, Sea Island truly can accommodate just about any dining request.

Chef Todd was most gracious to invite me to see his kitchens. He was very informative about the food from the island, explaining that the resort attempts to be as self-sufficient as possible. They bake their own breads daily and use local ingredients whenever possible. He introduced me to the muscadine. It looks like a giant blue grape, but the skin is very tough, so only the inner flesh is used. I tried some muscadine preserves that Chef Todd uses in a reduction sauce for wild boar. The two seemed to complement each other so well I wondered if perhaps the wild game could also be found on the island.

Chef Todd informed me that there is not only wild game on the island but that the island's managing company is very sensitive and committed to maintaining the region's resources. The St. Simon Land Trust was put into place by the island's first developer, Howard Coffin, in the late 1920s. As part of its provisions, a portion of the cost of every meal purchased at a resort restaurant goes toward protecting and maintaining nature and wildlife on the island.

We also bantered about our preferences for kitchen equipment, flexing our muscles, so to speak, when we came to discuss a certain cast-iron enameled stove. Chef Todd revealed the resort's plan to upgrade its restaurant and kitchen facilities as part of a huge renovation begun at The Cloister in 2004. The plan to systematically disassemble the famous Spanish Room located just off the main lobby and reassemble it when the new facility is completed shows the commitment Sea Island has for its honored past as well as its bright future.

Everywhere I went on the island I sensed the significant link between yesterday's and tomorrow's glories and traditions. It wasn't just found on the golf courses; it was alive in the very architecture, on the grounds of the resort complex, and in its policies concerning its natural resources. Chef Todd was not only a talented chef and an informative advocate

> A PORTION OF THE COST OF EVERY MEAL PURCHASED AT A RESORT RESTAURANT GOES TOWARD PROTECTING AND MAINTAINING NATURE AND WILDLIFE ON THE ISLAND.

for the resort's mission, but he was a darned nice guy, too. I really enjoyed cooking with him, our camaraderie, and his sense of humor.

For my second full day on Sea Island, I met up with Golf Pro Brannen Veal on the Plantation Course. Redesigned by Rees Jones in 1998, his course is classic in style and includes short finesse holes, strong par 4's and an unusual par 5 at the 18th hole. We had a great front 9. Brannen is a member of the Georgia PGA and playing with him provided a real opportunity to gain some valuable pointers. Though he never became distracted or lost composure on the course, I managed to break through his initially polite but reserved manner and discovered a really warm and genuinely funny guy.

really did stand alone in its views featuring the ocean panorama and the expansive promenade of massive live oaks covered by hanging moss. Not only did the landscape create a dramatic effect, but we also had high drama with our final shots. My drive off the tee landed just in front of the water. My second shot landed within 88 yards of the hole. I must credit Brannen's great golf tips for my vastly improved approach shots, as my third shot landed to the middle-right edge of the green. In two more putts, I was in for a solidly played par. There were high fives all around when Brannen eagled his long putt!

The Plantation Course embodies so much of Sea Island's character. I urge you to put this course on your wish list of must-play courses, and be sure to look for

THE PLANTATION COURSE EMBODIES SO MUCH OF SEA ISLAND'S CHARACTER.

At the 10th hole, I had to pause and take in the ocean backdrop and the Sidney Lanier Bridge within view off in the distance. The long par 4 started out strong, with a solid first hit to the 230-yard marker in the middle of the fairway. I grabbed a 3-wood for the next shot but missed, to the right of the bunker. I got out with a sand wedge and putted in with two strokes for a bogey.

Brannen worked with me on the next several holes, placing particular emphasis on my approach shots. His expert advice really did make a difference to my game. The 18th hole was such a memorable one, the hole couldn't have capped off the day's golf any better. It

Brannen. You'll count yourself lucky to play this course with a real pro like him.

In addition to its first-rate golf instruction, Sea Island also provides access to other activities available on the island, which are led by experts in various fields of interest. I had the pleasure of spending the afternoon with Sea Island's resident naturalist, Stacia Hendricks. We met at high tide. (Note: High tide is controlled by the lunar cycle, so check the current schedule for exact high tide times.) I was so intrigued by the salt marshes that I noticed on my drive from the mainland, I set out to kayak through the Marshes of Glynn with Stacia to get a closer look.

One of several fabulous courses on Sea Island, The Happy Isle.

We eased our kayaks into the water, and Stacia gave me some basic pointers on safety and how to maneuver the kayak before setting out to explore what she termed "nature's nursery ground." These saltwater marshes, Stacia explained, are the birthplaces of alligator, shrimp, oysters, and fish such as flounder, whiting, red fish and speckled trout. Dolphins have even been known to swim into the marshes. We passed a couple of guys returning from a crabbing expedition. Stacia told me that harvesting oysters, shrimp and blue crabs at the marshes is a popular activity for locals, as is sport fishing.

With the tide at its highest point, the water level covered the oyster beds and other sea life. The seafood nursery, teeming with culinary possibilities, would reveal itself when the water level dropped. Stacia was a wealth of information. She pointed out a holly tree, whose leaves and berries were once used by Native Americans to brew a caffeinic tea. She showed me a muscadine vine growing along the water's edge. After tasting the preserves in Chef Todd's kitchen, it was especially interesting to see the fruit growing wild.

An afternoon spent kayaking through the unfettered nature of the salt marshes is a nice complement to spending a morning on the golf course. Each evokes timelessness in its own way. Rather than trying to tame nature and model it to a human purpose as is the case in the game of golf, the voyage through the salt marshes fosters a sense of respect for the natural habitat. I felt privileged to witness this miraculous place where so many life forms get their start.

We paddled back to shore, literally into the sunset. It was spectacular in its pink and orange hues. After chatting so much about the area's indigenous foods, I was delighted to receive Stacia's generous gift. The jar of honey that she pulled out of her truck as we exchanged our good-byes is her own product, harvested from the bees she keeps on a nearby island. It was a perfect souvenir from my day with her.

I deliberately saved the most difficult course at Sea Island for my last day of golf. I summoned the confidence I had gained playing The Retreat Course, and the added advantage of Brannen's helpful instruction from our round on The Plantation Course, to gear up for Tom Fazio's windswept Seaside Course. The course's original nine holes were designed in the late-1920s by the noted London-based firm of Colt & Alison. These nine holes were held in high esteem even by the likes of Bobby Jones, who first played the course in 1920 and praised it as "one of the best nine holes I have ever seen." Impressive though they were, these nine holes did not match up well with the course's back nine. One of the strengths of Fazio's design from 1999 is that he created 18 seamless holes of golf.

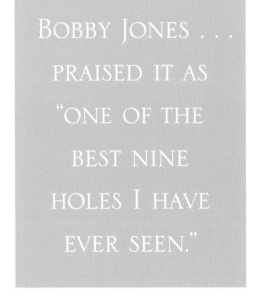

BOBBY JONES . . . PRAISED IT AS "ONE OF THE BEST NINE HOLES I HAVE EVER SEEN."

While playing, I really appreciated the course's cohesive feel and Fazio's artful design in the way each of the par 3's plays to a separate point of the compass. Holes 3 and 6 unfold counterclockwise while 12 and 17 on the in-9 play in the opposite direction. Seaside's 16th hole plays through the course's marshland section. It's a par 4 with water and marsh grasses on the left foreground and sweeping bunkers to the right and front on a raised green. The safe bet was to play it right and keep the ball out of the water. I kept my focus long enough to finish the hole before enjoying a last close-up look at the incredible marshlands. Thinking of what I learned with Stacia on the kayak excursion about all of the precious life forms at work here made the golf experience that much richer.

After sinking your feet into the turf of the three courses that are available for play at the Sea Island Golf Club and exploring the islands'

terrain and natural habitats, don't miss the opportunity to dine at Colt & Alison's at The Lodge. My meal here brought my visit to Sea Island back full circle, as echoes of Sea Island's past and golf's legends mingle with the here and now. The four-tiered seafood appetizer proudly showcased local shrimp, raw tuna, lobster, raw seasonal oysters served with a mignonette sauce, and lump crab meat. The selection of wines is vast, so I took the sommelier's suggestion to pair a wine flight with these delicacies and my snapper entrée, which was served with a ragout of andouille, clams, and new potatoes. For a final course before coffee, I savored the depth of flavors in a late-harvest riesling and its complementary full-mouth feel on the

SEA ISLAND HAS BEEN CALLED "THE HAPPY ISLE," AND IT'S NO WONDER, BECAUSE IT IS EASY TO FEEL YOUR STATE OF MIND IMPROVE WHILE YOU ARE HERE.

palate as it paired with a dense chocolate torte. I ended my final evening on Sea Island with the belief that I had indeed immersed myself in many of Sea Island's precious resources.

The people you will come in contact with at Sea Island, whether they are from the golf course and clubhouse, in the various dining establishments, or part of the hotel staff, are gracious and most hospitable. I felt so welcomed and so well cared for here. Even early morning wake-up calls came from a real person who asked if I would like a 15-minute snooze; now that's putting a human spin on the snooze button! Sea Island has been called "The Happy Isle," and it's no wonder, because it is easy to feel your state of mind improve while you are here.

SHRIMP SOUP WITH AÏOLI AND CROUTONS

RATING: A Long Par 4; High Greens Fees

SERVES: 10

After kayaking the Marshes of Glynn, where I passed right over countless shrimp beds, I wanted to create a dish that pulled out all of the goodness from this delicious local resource. The secret to making such a flavorful soup base is to cook the shrimp and vegetables in their entirety. Swirling the zesty flavors of the aïoli into the finished soup adds another dimension to the taste.

5 tablespoons olive oil	1 teaspoon Old Bay seasoning
2 1/4 pounds unpeeled whole shrimp	1 teaspoon herbes de Provence
2 large purple onions, chopped	1/4 cup sherry
2 pounds fresh tomatoes, chopped	1 bottle of white wine
2 tablespoons tomato paste	8 cups Vegetable Stock (page 181) or water
4 teaspoons shrimp paste	salt and freshly ground pepper to taste
1 fennel bulb, chopped	1 cup Aïoli (page 178)
1 garlic head, cut into halves	20 to 30 shrimp, cleaned and butterflied
1 pinch of saffron threads	20 croutons

Heat the olive oil in a large saucepan. Add the unpeeled shrimp and cook over high heat for 5 to 7 minutes, stirring constantly. Add the onions and sauté for 3 to 7 minutes longer or until the shrimp and onions are golden brown.

Add the tomatoes, tomato paste, shrimp paste, fennel, garlic, saffron, Old Bay seasoning and herbes de Provence. Add the sherry and white wine and cook until reduced by 1/2; you may also flambé the sherry if you prefer and allow the alcohol to cook off to rid the soup of a strong alcohol flavor.

Add enough Vegetable Stock to cover by 1 inch. Cook over medium heat for 1 1/2 hours. You may store in the refrigerator overnight at this point to fully develop the soup's flavor, if desired.

Press the warm soup through a ricer, straining out and reserving as much of the liquid as possible. If you do not have a ricer, you may process cooled soup in a food processor, then press it through a strainer to remove the liquid.

Return the reserved liquid to the saucepan and bring to a boil. Check the seasonings and season with salt and pepper. Remove 1 ladle of the mixture and combine with 1/4 cup of the Aïoli. Process in a blender and reserve for garnish.

Add the butterflied shrimp to the soup and cook for 1 to 2 minutes. Ladle the mixture into soup bowls and drizzle the reserved Aïoli mixture in a decorative circle over the surface. Serve with the remaining Aïoli and croutons.

TIP: Don't rush the process of searing the shrimp and vegetables; the more color you allow them to develop before adding the liquid, the more flavor the finished soup will have.

ENDIVE SALAD WITH TOASTED PECANS

RATING: A Gimme; Average Greens Fees

SERVES: 6

The sultry and spicy heat of the pecans livens this elegant salad. My recipe is simply a guide; adjust the amount of spice to your taste preferences and, by all means, refrain from using the piquant spices if they are too strong. You can always substitute cinnamon, a touch of nutmeg, or allspice when making the pecans.

8 heads of endive
salt and freshly ground pepper
   to taste
1/4 cup chopped chives
30 small teardrop or cherry tomatoes
1/2 cup Mustard Dressing (page 176)
1 cup Toasted Pecans (page 175)

Chop the endive heads and combine with salt and pepper to taste in a bowl. Add the chives, tomatoes and Mustard Dressing; toss to coat well.

Check the seasoning and spoon into a serving bowl or onto a serving plate. Sprinkle with the Toasted Pecans.

TIP: To ensure that you are purchasing the freshest produce, look for endives that are free of any brown leaves.

FRICASSEE OF CURRIED CHICKEN

RATING: Par for the Course on a Par 5; Low Greens Fees

SERVES: 4 to 6

A fricassee typically requires a long cooking time to develop its flavors, but in this recipe, the cooking process can be shortened, for the flavors of curry fully infuse into the chicken as it marinates overnight. The chicken will still develop its heady complexity in the shortened braising process. So enjoy an extra round of golf with this time-saver! The dish presents well when it's served individually or banquet-style on a platter.

Marinated Chicken
1 chicken
3 or 4 teaspoons curry powder
salt and freshly ground pepper to taste
4 garlic cloves
1/2 lemon, cut into 3 wedges
1/4 cup olive oil
2 tablespoons red wine vinegar

Fricassee
1 tablespoon curry powder
1 cup flour
salt and freshly ground pepper to taste
1/4 cup olive oil
1 carrot, coarsely chopped
1 onion, coarsely chopped
1 rib celery, coarsely chopped
4 cups Chicken Stock (page 179), simmering
bouquet garni of 1 sprig of thyme, 1 bay leaf
   and several parsley stems tied around
   a celery rib
2 tablespoons chopped fresh chives
2 tablespoons chopped fresh parsley

To marinate the chicken, rinse it inside and out and pat it dry. Season inside and out with the curry powder, salt and pepper. Place the garlic and lemon wedges in the cavity. Pour a mixture of the olive oil and vinegar over the chicken in a bowl. Marinate in the refrigerator for 8 hours or longer.

For the fricassee, remove the chicken from the marinade, discarding the lemon and garlic. Cut the chicken into 8 pieces and pat dry.

Mix the curry powder, flour, salt and pepper in a wide shallow bowl. Coat the chicken with the flour mixture, shaking off any excess.

Heat a large sauté pan and add a few tablespoons of the olive oil. Add only enough of the chicken to avoid crowding the pan and brown on all sides. Remove the chicken to a plate and repeat with the remaining olive oil and chicken.

Add the carrot, onion and celery to the sauté pan and sauté until light brown. Add a small amount of the Chicken Stock to the sauté pan and stir to deglaze the pan. Return the chicken to the pan and add enough of the remaining Chicken Stock to just cover the chicken. Place the bouquet garni in the pan.

Cook over low heat for 30 minutes, stirring frequently to cook evenly. Check for doneness and seasoning. Add the chives and parsley. Cook until the chicken is very tender.

TIP: Important flavors are contained in the browned bits on the bottom of the sauté pan. It is important to scrape up these bits with a wooden spoon when deglazing the pan with some of the chicken stock to add flavor to the fricassee.

HUGUENOT CHEESE SOUFFLÉ

RATING: Par for the Course on a Par 4; Low to Average Greens Fees

MAKES: 12 average portions or 8 to 10 family-style portions

What to do with an excess of egg whites? Make a soufflé! The French Huguenots who settled in the South introduced the rich gratins, soufflés, and cream desserts that continue to make up the Southern cook's repertoire. What may have begun as frugality has emerged as elegant comfort food. This recipe will work well if cut in half for six small portions or one large soufflé to feed four to six people. And don't panic; soufflés are easy to make and quite versatile.

> 1 cup (2 sticks) butter
> 1 cup flour
> 2 cups milk, heated
> 4 pinches of nutmeg
> salt and freshly ground white pepper to taste
> 2 whole eggs
> 1 3/4 cups (7 ounces) shredded Swiss cheese, or more to taste
> 1 cup (4 ounces) shredded Parmesan cheese, or more to taste
> 18 egg whites

Preheat the oven to 400 degrees. Butter and flour individual ramekins or a large soufflé dish.

Melt the butter in a saucepan. Stir in the flour with a wooden spoon and cook just until the flour is incorporated; do not allow to become darker than a buttery yellow. Whisk in the warmed milk and cook until the mixture is smooth and thickened, stirring constantly.

Remove from the heat and stir in the nutmeg, salt and pepper. Spoon into a large mixing bowl and whisk in the whole eggs and cheeses.

Beat the egg whites in a mixing bowl until medium-soft peaks form. Fold 1/4 of the egg whites into the cooked mixture; fold the remaining egg whites gradually into the mixture.

Fill the prepared dishes 3/4 full. Bake for 20 minutes for the individual ramekins, or for up to 40 minutes for the large soufflé dish; the soufflés should be puffed up beyond the rims of the dishes and brown on top.

Serve immediately, as the soufflés will quickly deflate.

TIP: To maintain the airiness of the egg whites, take care to fold them into the cooked mixture by moving the contents at the bottom of the bowl gently over the top of the mixture with a spatula. Any vigorous mixing in a clockwise direction will deflate the soufflé even before it begins to cook.

PLANTATION RICE

RATING: Par for the Course on a Par 4; Average Greens Fees

Serves 4 to 6

This rice dish, perfumed by curry powder, almonds and currants, is a toothsome pairing for the tender Fricassee of Curried Chicken (page 153).

1 tablespoon butter
1 onion, chopped
1³/4 cups uncooked rice
1 or 2 teaspoons mild curry powder
3 cups Chicken Stock (page 179) or Vegetable Stock (page 181), simmering
salt and freshly ground pepper to taste
1/2 cup roasted sliced almonds
1/2 cup currants
1 teaspoon butter

Preheat the oven to 350 degrees. Heat 1 tablespoon butter in an ovenproof saucepan and add the onion. Sauté until the onion is translucent. Add the rice and sauté until light brown.

Add the curry powder, stirring to coat the rice completely. Add the Chicken Stock and season with salt and pepper. Cover the saucepan and bake for 40 minutes or until the liquid has completely evaporated.

Add the almonds, currants and 1 teaspoon butter; stir to mix well and separate the grains.

TIP: Add a sliced banana or plantain to the rice if the curry flavor seems too strong.

CHOCOLATE PEACH CRUMBLE

RATING: Par for the Course on a Par 3; Average Greens Fees

SERVES: 6

Here's a twist on a classic Georgia dessert. After braising the peaches with the vanilla and butter, you might be tempted to stop right there; it's that delicious! By introducing a chocolate component, this crumble satisfies both the chocolate lover and those who steer toward fruit-based desserts. If peaches are out of season, try substituting a fruit that is at its peak of ripeness.

Filling
1/4 cup (1/2 stick) butter
5 large peaches, peeled and cut into quarters
1 tablespoon sugar
1 vanilla bean, split lengthwise
1/4 cup raisins
1/3 cup cream
1 egg
1 teaspoon sugar
1 teaspoon bourbon (optional)
3 ounces semisweet chocolate, grated

Topping
1/4 cup almond powder, made from finely
   ground blanched almonds
1/4 cup granulated sugar
1/4 cup flour
1/4 cup baking cocoa
1/4 cup (1/2 stick) butter
1/4 cup sliced almonds
confectioners' sugar, for garnish

Preheat the oven to 320 degrees. Butter a 9×13-inch baking dish.

For the filling, heat the butter in a large sauté pan. Add the peaches and sprinkle with 1 tablespoon sugar. Cook until the peaches begin to release their juices.

Add the vanilla bean and raisins. Cook for 5 to 8 minutes or until the fruit is tender but still holds it shape. Remove the vanilla bean and spoon the peach mixture into the prepared baking dish.

Combine the cream, egg, 1 teaspoon sugar and the bourbon in a mixing bowl and whisk until smooth. Pour over the fruit. Add the chocolate.

For the topping, combine the almond powder, granulated sugar, flour and baking cocoa in a bowl. Cut in the butter with a pastry cutter or 2 knives; the mixture should still contain lumps. Sprinkle over the filling and top with the sliced almonds.

Place the baking dish in a larger pan with water halfway up the side of the pan. Bake for 20 to 30 minutes or until golden brown. Garnish with confectioner's sugar and serve warm.

TIP: If you desire a really crunchy topping, broil for a minute or two before serving.

Photo for this recipe is on page 157.

GOLF AND TRADITION **SEA ISLAND**

56

PEANUT BUTTER CRÈME BRÛLÉE

RATING: Par for the Course on a Par 4; Average to High Greens Fees

SERVES: 4 to 6

Recipe for this photo is on page 156.

The playful pairing of peanut butter and celery gives this classic dessert a bit of whimsy. Have fun with this presentation.

4 to 6 teaspoons peanut butter
1/2 Crème Brûlée recipe (page 188), cooled
4 to 6 tablespoons sugar
1 rib celery, cut into sticks

Preheat the oven to 350 degrees. Whisk the peanut butter and cooled Crème Brûlée together in a bowl. Pour into individual ramekins. Place in a deep baking dish and pour boiling water around the ramekins to reach 2/3 up the side.

Bake for 20 minutes or just until the filling trembles when shaken. Cool to room temperature, wrap with plastic wrap and store in the refrigerator.

Sprinkle the sugar over the custards and caramelize with a food torch. Present the dessert with the celery sticks to break through the sugar topping and refresh the palate.

TIP: Make sure the peanut butter is at room temperature before combining it with the custard. If the peanut butter is too cold, it will separate from the custard while cooking.

The Oak Knoll Inn is a
peaceful bed-and-breakfast
nestled among 600 acres
of chardonnay vineyards.

NAPA

GOLFING IN WINE COUNTRY

VALLEY

California

In mid-March, I arrived to golf in the heart of wine country during Napa Valley's popular and well-attended Mustard Festival. Organized events aside, here in Napa, the real attraction is the land itself. A spate of warm weather had sent the valley and its vineyards into the full flowering of spring. There were mustard flowers in bloom all over the valley, carpeting the surrounding hillsides and filling in the rows of budding grape stock plantings with their bright-yellow brilliance. Nature is always putting on a spectacle, no matter what time of year it is, and when I visit wine country, I can't think of a better way to get the full experience of the land and the season than to stay as close as possible to the vineyards.

Tucked away just off Highway 29—the main thoroughfare running through Napa Valley—is Oak Knoll Inn. The quiet four-room bed-and-breakfast is fronted by a row of cypress trees and nestled in amongst 600 acres of chardonnay vineyards. Oak Knoll Inn's proprietor, Barbara Passino, greeted me with a glass of Champagne when I entered the inn's cozy common area. I was so charged up to be in the heart of wine country, a little bubbly was the perfect aperitif to kick off my stay!

We walked to the back deck from where we could take in views of the pool, the Jacuzzi, an arbor, and the magnificent vineyard setting. Each of the four doors on the deck leads to a private suite. Mine was comfortable and spacious, with fieldstone walls, a vaulted ceiling, and expansive windows that look out to the gardens and vineyards. The wood-burning fireplace in each room is a nice touch, too.

One of Barbara's many personal touches that she provides her guests are itineraries tailor-made to fit their interests. She and her staff will organize and make reservations for wine tours, deliver picnic lunches to picturesque grounds open to visitors at many of Napa's wineries, and plan bike tours or even a hot air balloon ride. I, however, was already set on following the perfect itinerary for a wine-country golf getaway created by Napa's own, "Mr. Golf," Mitch Cosentino, an acquaintance and kindred spirit, who is a winemaker by profession and a passionate golfer as a way of life. You won't find anyone in the valley who is more knowledgeable about Napa's golf courses.

I found Mitch hard at work in his office at Cosentino Winery, planning an upcoming golf tournament for a group of golfing friends from as far away as Japan. He excitedly described this year's golf event set to take place just down the road at The Vintner's Club and added his high hopes for his chosen site for next year's golf tournament at Eagle Vines, a new course adjacent to Napa's Chardonnay Club. Mitch's enthusiasm is contagious, and it's no wonder he feels such an affinity for these Napa courses; after all, they embody the two things he holds dear, golf and wine.

I could tell that we saw eye-to-eye on quite a number of subjects. Mitch's attitude about making wine is much like a chef's attitude about cooking. Chefs don't just make one dish; rather, they enjoy cooking a huge variety of things. In the kitchen, I am constantly refining and taking new inspiration from the foods that I use. Mitch takes pride in the more than 30 styles of wine he produces at Cosentino. Considering how much golf he plays, Mitch's energy is boundless. He personally tastes the contents of every barrel produced and decides when and how the wines will be bottled. He doesn't like to rush this process, either, claiming that deciding a wine's fate just after pressing is like predicting what a three-year-old will do for a living! Mitch is certainly a colorful guy, given to humorous metaphors. Don't let his affable way fool you; Mitch takes his craft seriously, and it's at the blending stage when Mitch really works his magic.

We toured his aging rooms, starting in the white room. We barrel-tasted a 2003 chardonnay that had been left on the lees. Letting the wine remain in contact with the pulverized grape dregs produced a juice with a wonderful scent and a lot of fruit. Mitch is proud of his chardonnay which he makes in the style of a premier cru chablis. It is not overtly oaky, and he doesn't resort to the addition of malic acid like so many producers of chardonnay do. Even at this early stage, it was already clear that the heavy fruit would give way in time to produce a regal chardonnay, rather than a "vanilla milk shake," as Mitch would say!

Continuing to barrel-taste his chardonnay wines, I gained a sense of the nuances that Mitch brings out in his blending and aging processes. We tasted the same wine that had not been left on the lees but had been aged in a different-style barrel. Its mineral character was much more predominant. Back in the tasting room, Mitch's 2002 CEV2 Chardonnay really impressed me. The mineral notes previewed a bright wine with a lot of intensity. This is a sophisticated wine whose style is leading the way in a trend in this region to produce more refined chablis-style chardonnays.

I have been a longtime fan of Cosetino's Poet Meritage wines, so I was especially interested in seeing what Mitch was working on in his red barreling rooms.

fermentation process, when the grape skins are mixed with the pressed juice that has been introduced to yeast. Three to four times daily for six to ten days, the cap is manually submerged to push the floating skins into the juice. Following this process, the fermented juice is placed in oak barrels for aging.

Each barrel we sampled exhibited a subtle difference in character. One was redolent with blackberries,

Most of the courses in Napa are surrounded by acres and acres of vineyards—a unique setting for any golfer.

NAPA VALLEY *Wine Country*

He was really excited about the grapes from Hoopes Ranch that would go into his 2002 cabernets and provide the backbone to these full-bodied wines. While we tasted a few barrel samples, Mitch explained why he prefers to work in small lots and described his use of punched-cap fermentation, a hands-on technique crucial to controlling the quality and character of his wines. The manual punching takes place during the

while another had spicy components. We tasted some of Mitch's bottled vintages from 2000 and 1999. They were almost chewy with such an abundance of fruit, but it was clear that over time, these cabs would mellow and evolve. Mitch has some exceptional wines in the making. Their complex flavors and aromas are products of his keen blending instincts and his dedication to staying involved in every step of the process.

After tasting so many wines, we were pretty hungry. Mitch suggested we eat at Hurley's in the center of Yountville. It's a favorite restaurant and watering hole for many of the vintners from Napa Valley. A side benefit of dining shoulder-to-shoulder with so many local wine makers here is the ability to choose from the wide selection of top Napa Valley wines that are limited in supply and typically hard to find. The plentiful supply of superb Napa wine pairs especially well with Chef Hurley's menu, with its emphasis on seasonal and local foods.

Since the weather was so warm, we sat outdoors on the patio under the shade of an olive tree and enjoyed Chef Bob Hurley's creations. We started with Mitch's favorite, a pancetta-wrapped quail and sausage brochette with warm cabbage salad. It was outstanding, as was the house-made ciabatta dunked in a swirl of fruity olive oil and balsamic vinegar, which our server deftly poured onto a plate table side. The chef poaches fresh locally caught tuna in olive oil for the pan bagnat sandwich. Combined with basil, tomato, baby lettuce, black olives, sliced hard-boiled egg, and sweet peppers, a bite of this sandwich for me is a mouthful of bright summers in the south of France. If you visit in the spring, like I did, don't miss his signature dessert, strawberry shortcake inspired by his mother's recipe.

On our way to golf, Mitch made a detour to The Vintner's Club, the site of his upcoming golf tournament. He couldn't resist the chance to show off this fun 9-hole course. I recommend this course, especially if you don't have a lot of time for golf while in Napa but need "a fix." With holes pushed up against fields of mustard flowers in bloom and surrounded by beautiful vineyards and mountains, this course offers both a beautiful setting and some challenges with its tournament tees.

The Chardonnay Club, however, might be Mitch's heaven on earth. Its three 9-hole courses and the new 18-hole Eagle Vines Course nearby are set within 140 acres of working vineyards, with another 200 acres of vineyards abutting the property. Not many scorecards list vineyards as out of bounds!

The San Francisco Bay links up to San Pablo Bay, which is visible off in the distance, and gives otters access to the grounds of the Chardonnay Club and Eagle Vines. Otters aren't the only animals that have been spotted. Coyotes, bobcats, rabbits, raccoons, osprey, egrets, eagles and blue jays are also in abundance. Though the course is new and in pristine condition, it has an established feeling largely due to the giant-size old California oaks that anchor the Eagle Vines clubhouse and factor into play on holes 1, 2, 17, and 18.

NOT MANY SCORECARDS LIST VINEYARDS AS OUT OF BOUNDS!

The remaining course is links style, with plenty of water hazards. Our afternoon play was brisk. Mitch knows the course and the game so well, he could instantly read the situation and make helpful suggestions along the way.

On 14, a par 3, a little stone bridge traverses a protected wetlands area. It turns out that its builder, who goes by the name of Scotty, built this as an exact replica of the original St. Andrews Bridge that he personally built in Scotland as a teen. Seeing this replica reminded me of Arnold Palmer's famous farewell to the world of professional golf, as he waved from the original St. Andrews Bridge in Scotland.

The next hole was a real challenge. At 580 yards, the long par 5 hits into the wind and up into a hill with a water hazard fronting the green. If you land right, you better have some extra balls, and if you're worried about the water, you had best play around it. Even though there's not one tree on this hole, it is still one of the toughest on the course.

As memorable and picturesque holes go, the island hole is top-notch. No matter what your golfing ability is, Mitch insists that you play the back tee. This gorgeous elevated tee box is set against a terraced rock retaining wall and plantings of flowers around a cascading waterfall. Approach this dramatic hole by crossing a little wooden bridge, and take a moment to enjoy the sweeping view that surveys all of the vineyards and the golf course. Mitch counseled me on my tee shot, explaining that he uses a pitching wedge when the wind is up or an 8- or 9-iron on calmer days. Today's pin placement was back on the green with a prevailing wind, so I grabbed my 3-iron, with Mitch's nod of approval.

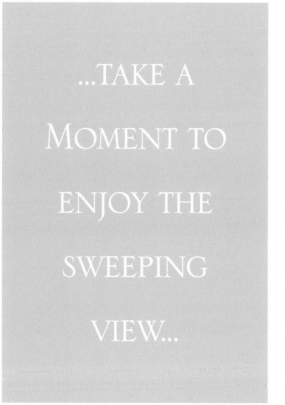

...TAKE A MOMENT TO ENJOY THE SWEEPING VIEW...

The 17th hole is the only one on Eagle Vines with a blind tee shot. Old California oaks factor into play here, as do the severe elevation changes, but Mitch remained optimistic and claimed the hole was birdie-able. That may be so for a scratch golfer like Mitch, but for a golfer like me, the uphill pitch shot was pretty tough. I was happy with a bogey. There's actually a 19th hole at the Chardonnay Club. At 75 yards, it's the perfect debt settler.

Playing golf surrounded by acres and acres of vineyards is truly unique. I can't say enough about this special setting. No matter when you might have the chance to come and experience the Chardonnay Club's and Eagle Vines' courses for yourself, your golf game here will stand out in your memory. Play here in the early spring when the vines are just budding or later when the hills are covered with bright flowers and the vines have filled in. The parched brown hills contrast with the lush vineyards of summer and turn to brilliant fall colors at harvest time.

The ever-changing grounds bring energy to the atmosphere and join two of my own life's passions, golf and wine, into a harmonious state.

Back at Oak Knoll Inn, I sipped some chardonnay while enjoying the peaceful sunset over the vineyards. Each evening, Barbara prepares a fantastic spread of cheese and hors d'oeuvre to accompany the revolving selection of wines that she features from local wineries. Vintners often come to her cocktail hour to present a tasting of their wines. Not only is this a pleasant gathering, but also it's a great way to learn about a specific winery and to ask questions of the actual wine makers, in a relaxed setting. After such a full day, it was nice to settle into the soothing atmosphere of Oak Knoll. The next day would be another jam-packed day of activity in Napa Valley.

Calistoga also shed some light on how the landscape in Napa Valley came to be carpeted each spring in brilliant yellow.

Calistoga's settlement by Spanish missionaries in the early 19th century is the key reason for the stunning mustard blossoms that bloom all across the valley. Local legend tells of Friar Jose Altimira, who came to Calistoga and planted the first grapevines in the region. He left a trail of mustard seeds behind him so that he would be able to find his way back to Calistoga in the spring when the mustard plants would blossom into their striking characteristic bright yellow blooms. The mustard seeds have since scattered and now cover the whole valley in their springtime splendor of color.

Turning south again on curvy Highway 128, I passed under a canopy of trees as I entered the quaint town

On the day I dined here, I spotted a certain ex-quarterback for the 49ers also enjoying a relaxing midday meal. I wonder what his golf handicap is?

I set out for the northernmost town in Napa Valley, Calistoga, known historically as "The Hot Springs of the West." While the geyser in this sleepy town plays quite an important role in science, for the layman like myself, it's a natural wonder that is simply awesome to behold. Old Faithful is a whole lot of hot water, but the town of Calistoga also produces delicious and refreshing sparkling and still water from its nearby natural mineral springs. Look for a bottle of the locally produced, crystal-clear Calistoga water to keep yourself well hydrated while wine tasting at the many wineries in Northern California. Besides discovering Calistoga's many liquid resources, my stop in

of St. Helena. For me, this is America with all of its small- town charm. It is also home to the Culinary Institute of America, one of the top cooking schools in the country. I walked down Main Street for a little window-shopping, and then enjoyed lunch at Martini House. It is located in a Spanish colonial home on Spring Street, just off the main drag. The outdoor space with gardens and a small fountain is meticulously maintained, and the food is sophisticated and delicious. On the day I dined here, I spotted a certain ex-quarterback for the 49ers also enjoying a relaxing midday meal. I wonder what his golf handicap is?

Just south of St. Helena on Highway 29 is the town of Rutherford, where I made a stop at the St. Helena Olive Oil Company. They offer a complete sampling of their 2004 Napa Valley extra-virgin olive oil harvest at their tasting bar inside their retail store. Like its sister wine industry, the high-quality first-cold-pressed olive oils range in flavors from fruity blends to varietals with a nutty profile. The top notes can be herbaceous and grassy or turn spicy with a final kick to the back of the throat. The olive harvest takes place in the fall, with a late harvest in December and January. Late-harvested olive oil does not have the intense fruity olive characteristics of the earlier harvested olives, but it pairs quite well with lemon oil. Think of this as the olive oil equivalent of the concentrated flavors of a late-harvest dessert wine.

I am sorry to report that as of yet, there are no plans for any golf courses at Copia. I'll have to get Mitch working on it!

Inside Copia, a tremendous amount of space is devoted to permanent and revolving art exhibitions, all of which take some aspect of food and wine as their inspiration. Films and lectures occur regularly in the 260-seat theater. Just like the Napa Valley, Copia is a busy place. You can even saunter over to their wine-tasting table to sample and learn about wines from all across the United States. Copia's mission, "to educate, promote, and celebrate American excellence and achievements in the culinary, wine-making, and visual arts," is the vision of longtime Napa resident and wine-maker Robert Mondavi. Copia's dedication to celebrating America's rich culinary and artistic

Copia's mission, "to educate, promote, and celebrate American excellence and achievements in the culinary, wine-making, and visual arts," is the vision of longtime Napa resident and wine-maker Robert Mondavi.

As a final stop on my Napa Valley journey, I headed for Copia: The American Center for Wine, Food & the Arts. Opened in 2001, and located right in Napa's downtown district at First Street, Copia is a microcosm of Napa Valley itself. There are expansive gardens to explore, with seasonal plantings of fruits, vegetables, herbs, and flowers that are used in cooking demonstrations at Copia's tiered-kitchen forum and in its restaurant, Julia's Kitchen, named after Copia's honorary trustee, Julia Child. Orchards, vineyards, and a 500-seat grass concert terrace facing the Napa River complete the 12 acres of grounds.

heritage makes for a meaningful experience. Come here as a way to orient yourself to the Napa Valley or as a final cap to an amazing Napa Valley journey.

Wherever your interests lie, be sure to stop at Cosentino Winery for a comprehensive introduction to stellar Napa Valley wine. Give Mitch my regards, and if he's not hard at work on the job, you can bet he's hard at play at the Vintner's Club course, at Eagle Vines, or next door on one of the 27 holes at the Chardonnay Club. Follow his lead and experience Napa Valley in all its glory, surrounded by thriving vineyards and lots of great golf.

GREEN OLIVE AND BACON MUFFINS

RATING: Par for the Course on a Par 3; Average Greens Fees

MAKES: 18 muffins; 45 miniature muffins

In addition to its extensive wine industry, Napa Valley produces a variety of olives that are pressed to make olive oils or cured for the table. Big green table olives, like the picholine, that are full of nutty and fruity flavors make great additions to a basic muffin. These muffins are delicious first thing in the day or as an accompaniment to a meal. The balance of olive and crumb is a personal preference, so it you like a chunkier, more rustic muffin, with the assurance of an olive slice in each bite, double the quantity of olives in the batter.

2 cups flour
2 tablespoons baking powder
1 1/4 teaspoons salt
1 1/4 cups (2 1/2 sticks) butter, softened
1 1/2 cups plus 1 tablespoon sugar
1/4 teaspoon vanilla extract
5 eggs
2/3 cup milk
3 slices bacon, crisp-cooked and crumbled
24 picholine olives, pitted and sliced

Sift the flour, baking powder and salt together. Cream the butter, sugar and vanilla in a mixing bowl until light and fluffy. Beat in the eggs 1 at a time at low speed. Add the milk in a steady stream, beating constantly.

Add the sifted dry ingredients 1/3 at a time, mixing at low speed after each addition. Let the batter rest in the refrigerator for 1 hour.

Preheat the oven to 350 degrees. Reserve 1/3 of the crumbled bacon and fold the remaining bacon into the batter with the sliced olives. Spoon the mixture into greased muffin cups, filling the cups halfway. Sprinkle the reserved bacon on top of the batter.

Bake for about 25 minutes for regular muffins or for 10 to 15 minutes for miniature muffins, or until the muffins are golden brown and a wooden pick inserted into the center comes out clean. Remove to a rack to cool.

BAY SCALLOPS AND OYSTER FRICASSEE WITH ORGANIC CUCUMBERS

RATING: Par for the Course on a Par 4; High Greens Fees

SERVES: 4

The Bay area is a rich resource for shellfish, and Napa Valley's temperate climate supports a strong agricultural industry that goes well beyond its famed wine and olives. Produce from this region, like tomatoes and cucumbers, is loaded with sun-ripened flavor. When selecting seasonal produce from your region, use your sense of smell to help find the most desirable item, and choose fruits and vegetables that feel heavy for their size. They will be juicy and very flavorful.

1 tablespoon butter
1 onion, finely chopped
2 plum tomatoes, seeded and chopped
2 organic cucumbers, seeded and finely chopped
2 garlic cloves, minced
salt and freshly ground pepper to taste
2 cups white wine, such as chardonnay
12 bay scallops, shucked and rinsed in cold water
4 oysters, shucked with the liquor reserved and
   the oysters rinsed in cold water
1 tablespoon chopped fresh tarragon, for garnish

Heat a medium sauté pan. Add the butter, onion, tomatoes, cucumbers and garlic. Sauté until the cucumbers and onions begin to be tender and sprinkle with salt and pepper.

Add the white wine to the sauté pan and cook until the alcohol evaporates, stirring to deglaze the pan; quite a lot of liquid will remain in the pan.

Add the scallops and the oysters with their liquor. Cook for just a couple of minutes. Garnish with the tarragon and serve.

TIP: This requires some strength and fortitude to shuck the oysters. It also requires a little finesse at the last stage of cooking, as the oysters and scallops cook really fast. Consider that the hot liquid will continue to cook the shellfish even after everything has been removed from the heat. Once the shellfish turn opaque, it is time to remove the dish from the heat, or the shellfish will become tough.

SAUTÉED FRESH FOIE GRAS WITH VERJUS AND GRAPES

RATING: Par for the Course on a Par 3; High Greens Fees

SERVES: 4

A grand starter course, foie gras is actually relatively easy to prepare. Your biggest challenge for this dish may be in procuring all of the ingredients. Check your specialty stores or try on-line resources. Verjus is the acidic juice extracted from large unripe white grapes and their musts. It is similar to vinegar, as it does not contain any alcohol.

> *4 (2-ounce) slices foie gras*
> *salt and freshly ground pepper to taste*
> *16 medium grapes, peeled and seeded*
> *1/4 cup verjus*
> *1/4 cup Vegetable Stock (page 181)*

Season the foie gras on both sides with salt and pepper. Heat a large sauté pan and sear the foie gras in the pan until it is caramelized brown on both sides. Remove the foie gras and add the grapes to the pan.

Add the verjus and Vegetable Stock and cook over medium-high heat until the liquid is reduced by 1/2, stirring up the browned bits from the bottom of the pan with a wooden spoon. Check and adjust the seasoning.

Pour the cooking liquid and grapes over the foie gras. Serve with mixed greens.

TIP: For a peppery accent and your own Napa Valley-inspired springtime dish, add some baby mustard greens or arugula to the mixed greens and garnish with bright yellow edible flower petals from the mustard plant or marigold.

VEAL MEDALLIONS WITH VEGETABLES AND HORSERADISH RED WINE SAUCE

RATING: A Long Par 4; High Greens Fees

SERVES: 4

All of the fantastic wines I tasted at Cosentino Winery inspired me to include this dish, which features a horseradish-infused red wine sauce. Cheers, Mitch!

12 snow peas
4 scallions
4 baby carrots
12 small cauliflower florets
8 hearts of palm
4 slices zucchini
4 slices yellow squash
3 tablespoons peas
4 (3-ounce) veal medallions
salt and freshly ground
    pepper to taste
3 tablespoons olive oil
1/4 cup Vegetable Stock
    (page 181)
3 1/2 tablespoons Soy Sauce
    Butter (page 182)
1/2 cup Red Wine Sauce
    (page 183)
1 tablespoon freshly
    grated horseradish
1 tablespoon butter

Preheat the oven to 400 degrees. Bring a stockpot of water to a boil and blanch the snow peas, scallions, carrots, cauliflower, hearts of palm, zucchini, yellow squash and peas separately; the vegetables should remain crisp. Plunge the vegetables into an ice water bath to stop the cooking process.

Season the veal with salt and pepper. Heat a medium ovenproof saucepan to smoking over high heat. Add the olive oil and sear the veal medallions on both sides.

Place the saucepan in the oven and roast to 145 degrees on a meat thermometer for medium. Remove the veal and let rest.

Heat the Vegetable Stock in a medium sauté pan. Add all the blanched vegetables except the peas. Cook until reduced to the desired consistency; add the peas and cook just until heated through. Stir in the Soy Sauce Butter and season with salt and pepper.

Combine the Red Wine Sauce and horseradish in a small saucepan. Cook over medium-high heat to infuse the flavor. Remove from the heat and swirl in the butter.

Place the veal medallions in the centers of 4 serving plates. Spoon the vegetables along the edges of the plates and drizzle the Red Wine Sauce over the veal and vegetables.

FLOUNDER WITH TOMATO-FENNEL FONDUE AND BROWN BUTTER

RATING: A Long Par 5; Average Greens Fees

SERVES: 4

Cooking the vegetables over low heat for a long time will concentrate their pure flavors and create a pulpy sauce called a fondue. It's a fine pairing for the light, but buttery, brown butter sauce spooned over the fish. Making brown butter is a bit like putting on a fast green; sometimes it's a smart idea to hold back a little to allow for the extra roll. In this case, the "extra roll" is the cooking that occurs when the food traps in the heat and continues to cook even after it has been removed from the direct heat.

Tomato-Fennel Fondue
3 tablespoons olive oil
2 whole shallots
cloves of 2 garlic heads
1 head of fennel, sliced
4 tomatoes, seeded and chopped
salt and freshly ground pepper to taste
1/2 cup white wine
1/2 cup Vegetable Stock (page 181)

Brown Butter Sauce
1/2 cup (1 stick) unsalted butter
juice of 1 lemon

Flounder
4 (4- to 6-ounce) flounder fillets
salt and freshly ground pepper
olive oil

For the fondue, warm the olive oil in a small saucepan over low heat. Add the shallots, garlic, fennel and tomatoes and sweat until very tender; the vegetables should release their liquid but should not brown. Season with salt and pepper.

Increase the heat to medium-high and add the wine. Cook until the liquid is reduced by 1/2, stirring up the browned bits from the bottom of the pan. Add the Vegetable Stock and cook until the fondue has a pulpy consistency.

For the brown butter, melt the unsalted butter in a small saucepan over low heat. Cook until the butter is brown and releases a nutty aroma; don't be afraid to pull the saucepan off the heat a little early if you are in doubt, as it will continue to brown. Whisk in the lemon juice, taking care not to splatter the hot butter.

For the flounder, season the fillets on both sides with salt and pepper. Sear in a small amount of olive oil in a skillet for about 3 minutes on each side or until cooked through.

To serve, place the fillets on serving plates and drizzle with the Brown Butter. Spoon the Tomato-Fennel Fondue onto the plates.

TIP: Holding back a little of the cooking time until you get a feel for making a brown butter sauce could keep it from burning. If you determine that the butter needs a little more time over the flame, feel free to return it to the heat; there's no penalty stroke in cooking!

Asian Mustard Spaetzle

RATING: A Short Par 4; Low Greens Fees

SERVES: 4

Enjoy this spaetzle with the Veal Medallions on page 170. Its mustard component really plays off the veal's soy- and horseradish-based sauce. To prepare a plain spaetzle, simply omit both mustards, or create your own signature spaetzle by adding your own original flavors.

8 cups water
2 eggs
1/2 cup water
1/2 teaspoon salt
1 1/2 cups flour
1/2 tablespoon mustard seeds
1 1/2 tablespoons hot Asian mustard
1/4 teaspoon herbes de Provence (optional)
2 tablespoons vegetable oil
2 tablespoon butter

Bring 8 cups water to a boil in a large stockpot. Beat the eggs with 1/2 cup water and the salt in a mixing bowl. Whisk in the flour gradually to make a batter. Stir in the mustard seeds, Asian mustard and herbes de Provence.

Use my preferred method to form the spaetzle by placing the batter in a pastry bag fitted with a medium top and squeezing droplets of the batter into the boiling water in batches; you may also press the batter through a colander with large holes into the boiling water, if preferred.

Cook the spaetzle until it rises to the top of the water, stirring with a slotted spoon and giving any that stick to the bottom of the pot a gentle push. Remove the cooked spaetzle with the slotted spoon to drain. Repeat the process with the remaining batter.

Heat a large sauté pan and add the oil and butter. Sauté the drained spaetzle in the oil mixture until golden brown and serve.

Petite Chocolate Cakes with Coffee Essence

RATING: Par for the Course on a Par 3; Average Greens Fees

SERVES: 8 (or 4 chocoholics)

Barbara Passino's sumptuous and decadent chocolate tacos that she serves for breakfast at Oak Knoll Inn set a tone for starting the day with a fortifying and indulgent meal. For those who are certified chocoholics, these bite-size cakes might be your idea of the perfect start to a day; after all, there is coffee in them! For the rest of you, enjoy these cakes, with their molten chocolate middles, at the end of a meal.

1/2 cup (1 stick) unsalted butter
flour
3/4 cup chopped semisweet chocolate
3 whole eggs
3 egg yolks
1/3 cup sugar
1 to 4 tablespoons coffee extract,
    depending on desired strength of coffee flavor
2/3 cup flour

Butter individual ramekins with some of the butter and dust with flour. Place in the refrigerator until needed. Chop the remaining butter.

Melt the chocolate in a double boiler. Add the chopped butter and heat until the butter melts, stirring to blend well.

Whisk the whole eggs in a bowl. Add to the chocolate mixture. Beat the egg yolks with the sugar in a bowl and stir gently into the chocolate mixture. Stir in the coffee extract. Add 2/3 cup flour and mix well.

Spoon the mixture into the prepared ramekins without filling to the rim. Chill in the refrigerator for 1 1/2 hours; for the ultimate taste, it is best to bake them just before serving.

Preheat the oven to 375 degrees. Bake the cakes for about 15 minutes or until they are crisp on the outside but runny in the center. Pair these rich and pleasantly bittersweet cakes with a crème anglaise or even a dollop of vanilla ice cream.

TIP: A double boiler is the key to making this mixture. If you don't own one, you can simulate one by placing a medium metal mixing bowl over a saucepan of heated water. The water should not boil or touch the bottom of the bowl; you want a gentle, but constant, heat for melting and incorporating the ingredients.

THE
PRO SHOP
Essentials

SIMPLE SYRUP

RATING: A Gimme; Low Greens Fees

MAKES: About 2¹/₂ cups

Simple syrup is great to have on hand for many uses, including frostings, as a sweetener for cold beverages, and as a versatile base for mixed drinks. It keeps in the refrigerator indefinitely.

2 cups sugar
2 cups water

Combine the sugar and water in a small saucepan. Bring to a rapid boil over medium-high heat, stirring to dissolve the sugar completely. Remove from the heat immediately.

Cool to room temperature. Transfer to a plastic container and store, covered, in the refrigerator.

TOASTED PECANS

RATING: A Gimme: Average Greens Fees

MAKES: 1 cup

This recipe can be used with other nuts. Because pecans have a high oil content, they burn easily. Consequently, cooking times are far shorter for pecans than for other nuts. The chili powder and curry powder create some of their own heat. By all means, adjust the seasonings to accommodate your preferences.

1 cup pecan halves
¹/₄ teaspoon chili powder
¹/₄ teaspoon coriander powder
¹/₄ teaspoon curry powder

1¹/₂ tablespoons melted butter
2 tablespoons granulated sugar
2 tablespoons brown sugar

Preheat the oven to 350 degrees. Mix the pecans, chili powder, coriander powder, curry powder and melted butter in a bowl and toss to mix well.

Heat a sauté pan and add the pecan mixture. Sprinkle with the sugars and mix well with a wooden spoon; the pecans will be lumpy. Sauté for 2 to 3 minutes.

Spread the pecans on a baking sheet. Bake for 4 to 5 minutes or until the pecans are fragrant, stirring once.

Cool to room temperature. Store in an airtight container for up to 3 days. Do not store in the refrigerator, as the coating will become soggy.

TIP: The pecans are done when they become fragrant in the cooking process. Use this easy rule of thumb—or nose, in this case—for any nut you choose to use. Other nuts may require additional cooking time, so use your sense of smell to check for doneness.

BALSAMIC VINAIGRETTE

RATING: A Gimme; Average Greens Fees

MAKES: 1 1/2 cups or 1 cruet

1 1/4 cups olive oil
1/2 cup balsamic vinegar
1 tablespoon chopped shallots
1 tablespoon chopped chives
salt and freshly ground pepper to taste

Combine the olive oil, vinegar, shallots and chives in a blender and process until smooth. Season with salt and pepper to taste. Store in the refrigerator.

MUSTARD DRESSING

RATING: A Gimme; Low Greens Fees

MAKES: 1 1/2 cups or 1 cruet

The mustard and vinegar "cook" the egg yolk, which is a vital component to this rich and glossy dressing. The egg yolk brings richness to the dressing and prevent it from separating.

1 egg yolk*
1 tablespoon warm water
1/4 cup Dijon mustard
1 cup olive oil
1 tablespoon red wine vinegar, or to taste
salt and freshly ground pepper to taste

Combine the egg yolk, water and Dijon mustard in the bowl of a mixer fitted with a whip attachment; mix at low speed. Increase the speed to high and add the olive oil in a steady stream, mixing constantly until the mixture has the consistency of mayonnaise.

Blend in the vinegar and season with salt and pepper. Store in the refrigerator.

TIP: To repair a broken dressing, whisk in one egg yolk and a little water. Like a patch over a small divot on the tee box, the damage will never be noticed. Conversely, if the dressing is too thick, thin it out by adding a touch more warm water.

*To avoid the danger of salmonella in uncooked eggs, you can use an equivalent amount of pasteurized egg substitute.

Ravigote Dressing

RATING: A Gimme; Average Greens Fees

MAKES: 2 cups

The raw egg yolks are "cooked" by the acidic ingredients added to this dressing. If you are uncomfortable using uncooked egg yolks, you can omit them from the recipe. The end result will still have plenty of body and richness.

1 bunch parsley
6 stalks tarragon
11 stems chervil
1/4 cup drained capers
1/3 cup cornichons
3 egg yolks
1 tablespoon red wine vinegar
1/4 cup Dijon mustard
1 tablespoon (or more) cornichon juice
1 cup olive oil

Combine the parsley, tarragon and chervil in a food processor and process to chop well. Add the capers and cornichons and pulse to chop; scrape down the side of the container.

Add the egg yolks, vinegar, Dijon mustard and 1 tablespoon cornichon juice. Drizzle the olive oil through the feed tube slowly, processing constantly to emulsify.

Adjust the consistency of the dressing if it appears too thick by adding a bit more cornichon juice. Store in the refrigerator.

TIP: The dressing made with the egg yolks will keep for up to 1 week in the refrigerator. If made without the egg yolks, it will keep for several weeks.

TRUFFLE VINAIGRETTE

RATING: A Gimme; High Greens Fees

MAKES: About 1¼ cups or 1 cruet

Truffle oil is bold in flavor and aroma, but it fetches a real premium at the market. To highlight this rare specialty, pair it with a salad of delicate baby lettuces at their prime.

1 cup truffle oil
2 tablespoons red wine vinegar
2 tablespoons sherry vinegar

2 tablespoons water
1 teaspoon salt
¹/₂ teaspoon freshly ground pepper

Combine the truffle oil, red wine vinegar, sherry vinegar, water, salt and pepper in a bowl or blender; mix or process until emulsified. Adjust the seasonings and store in the refrigerator.

AÏOLI

RATING: A Short Par 3; Average to High Greens Fees

MAKES: 1 cup

Aïoli is the perfect accompaniment to fish- and seafood-based stews and soups. Aïoli's vibrant flavors and sunny yellow color radiate its warmth. It's beautiful drizzled in soup or slathered on a crouton for a bolder taste.

¹/₄ cup water
1 or 2 garlic cloves, minced
1 pinch saffron threads
1 teaspoon Dijon mustard

1 egg*
1 cup olive oil
salt and freshly ground pepper to taste

Combine the water with the garlic and saffron threads in a sauté pan and heat to release the flavors. Remove to a blender and add the Dijon mustard and egg.

Add the olive oil in a steady stream, processing constantly to emulsify. Season with salt and pepper. Spoon into an airtight container and store in the refrigerator for up to 1 week.

*To avoid the danger of salmonella in uncooked eggs, you can use an equivalent amount of pasteurized egg substitute.

CHICKEN STOCK

RATING: A Long Par 4; Low Greens Fees

MAKES: About 1 gallon

Instead of discarding chicken bones, freeze them until you are ready to make a stock. Your butcher is another good source for obtaining bones. They may cost only pennies, but the chicken carcasses are valuable for their flavor and the natural gelatin needed to create a superior stock.

10 pounds chicken carcasses
1 large unpeeled onion, coarsely chopped
2 medium carrots, peeled and coarsely chopped
2 ribs celery, coarsely chopped
1 garlic head, cut into halves crosswise
2 bay leaves
2 sprigs thyme
2 sprigs parsley
2 tablespoons black peppercorns

Preheat the oven to 400 degrees. Rinse the chicken carcasses and pat them dry. Place them in a large roasting pan. Roast for 1 1/2 hours or until very brown.

Remove the bones to a very large stockpot. Pour off any excess fat from the roasting pan. Add enough water to the pan to deglaze it, scraping up any browned bits from the bottom of the pan. Add the water and browned bits to the stockpot.

Add the onion, carrots, celery, garlic, bay leaves, thyme, parsley, peppercorns and enough additional water to cover the ingredients by 2 or 3 inches. Bring to a boil over medium-high heat. Reduce the heat and simmer for 4 to 5 hours, skimming the surface occasionally.

Strain the mixture through a fine sieve, pressing out as much liquid as possible. Cool the stock in an ice water bath. Store in the refrigerator.

TIP: Any remaining fat in the stock will congeal on top when it is chilled. It can then be easily removed, and the remaining stock should be clear.

VEAL STOCK

RATING: A Long Par 4; Average Greens Fees

MAKES: About 5 quarts

Making stock doesn't have to be a lonely, time-consuming task. Spend your precious leisure time in a productive and socially relaxing way by planning a stock-making party around a Master's Tournament, a Super Bowl, or other big televised event. While the stock is simmering, you and your friends can sit back, sip some wine, and enjoy. When your guests leave, they can each take some stock home with them.

12 pounds veal bones
1 bottle good inexpensive burgundy,
    plus additional for deglazing the pan
1 large onion, coarsely chopped
1 large carrot, coarsely chopped
4 ribs celery, coarsely chopped
2 garlic heads, separated into unpeeled cloves
2/3 cup tomato paste
4 bay leaves
4 sprigs thyme
1 bunch parsley
1 tablespoon black peppercorns

Preheat the oven to 450 degrees. Place the veal bones in a large roasting pan and roast for 35 minutes or until well browned on all sides. Remove the bones to a large stockpot and add 1 bottle of wine. Cook until reduced by 1/2, skimming the surface occasionally.

Pour off any excess fat from the roasting pan and add the onion, carrot, celery and garlic. Roast until the vegetables are caramelized. Stir in the tomato paste and cook for about 5 minutes. Add the vegetable mixture to the stockpot.

Add additional wine to the roasting pan, stirring up the browned bits from the bottom of the pan with a wooden spoon. Add to the stockpot. Add the bay leaves, thyme, parsley, peppercorns and enough water to cover the ingredients by 3 inches.

Bring to a boil, and skim the surface. Reduce the heat to low and simmer for 4 hours. Remove the bones and strain the stock, pressing out as much liquid as possible. Store the stock in the refrigerator or freezer.

Vegetable Stock

RATING: A Short Par 3; Low Greens Fees

MAKES: About 1 gallon

Most stocks are time-consuming to make, but vegetable stock is the exception. It is a fast and easy staple to make and wonderful to have on hand. Freeze it in small quantities for use in everyday cooking.

2 yellow onions, coarsely chopped
2 large carrots, peeled and coarsely chopped
3 ribs celery, coarsely chopped
1/2 garlic head
1 leek, washed and chopped
1 tomato, chopped
1 zucchini, chopped
1 bay leaf
1 sprig thyme
2 sprigs parsley
1 tablespoon black peppercorns

Combine the onions, carrots, celery, garlic, leek, tomato and zucchini in a large stockpot. Add the bay leaf, thyme, parsley, peppercorns and enough cold water to cover the ingredients by 3 to 4 inches.

Bring to a boil over medium-high heat. Reduce the heat and simmer for 30 minutes. Strain the stock, discarding the vegetables. Cool the stock in an ice water bath and store in the refrigerator or freezer.

TIP: Leave the skins on the onions to add color to the stock.

GARLIC BUTTER

RATING: Par for the Course on a Par 3; Low Greens Fees

MAKES: 1 cup

In my experience, garlic butter is the handiest of all compound butters to keep in your kitchen repertoire. It can add a lot of pizzazz to anything from a steak to vegetables to starchy dishes. The method is simple enough, so use this recipe as a primer and develop some of your own winning combinations.

1/2 cup (1 stick) butter, softened
1/2 bunch parsley, finely chopped
1 clove garlic, minced

Combine the butter, garlic and parsley in a bowl; mix with a wooden spoon until smooth. Spoon into a storage container and store in the refrigerator.

TIP: Shape the butter into a log, wrap in plastic wrap and store in the freezer for longer periods, and to have on hand for topping steaks.

SOY SAUCE BUTTER

RATING: A Gimme; Low Greens Fees

MAKES: About 1 cup

4 cups soy sauce
1/4 cup (2 ounces) sugar
1 cup (2 sticks) butter, softened

Combine the soy sauce and sugar in a small saucepan. Cook until reduced by 1/2. Let stand until cool.

Combine the soy sauce reduction with the butter in a mixing bowl and mix with the whip attachment until smooth.

Red Wine Sauce

RATING: Par for the Course on a Par 4; Average Greens Fees

MAKES: 1 quart

When cooking with wine, choose a good quality one, something that you would also enjoy drinking. The wine does not need to be expensive, but avoid products marked "cooking wine," which are loaded with salt and are unsuitable for cooking as well as for straight consumption.

> 2 tablespoons olive oil
> 1 cup chopped onion
> 1/2 cup chopped carrots
> 1/2 cup chopped celery
> 1/2 head garlic, chopped
> 8 ounces roasted veal or chicken bones
> 4 sprigs thyme
> 1 tablespoon herbes de Provence
> 1 tablespoon black peppercorns
> 4 cups red wine
> 4 cups Veal Stock (page 180)

Heat the olive oil in a saucepan. Add the onion, carrots, celery, garlic, roasted bones, thyme, herbes de Provence and peppercorns and sweat over low heat until the vegetables are translucent but not browned.

Add the wine and heat over medium-high heat until reduced by 1/2, stirring up the browned bits from the bottom of the saucepan. Add the Veal Stock and cook until reduced to a consistency that will coat the back of a spoon.

Strain through a fine mesh strainer into a storage container. Store in the refrigerator.

FRESH PASTA

RATING: A Long Par 4; Average Greens Fees

SERVES: 8

This delicate pasta is best served with some freshly grated Parmesan cheese and paired with shellfish or breast of chicken.

1 cup chopped mixed fresh parsley, tarragon,
   chives and chervil
18 egg yolks
1¼ to 1½ cups (or more) flour
½ tablespoon salt
1 teaspoon olive oil
salt to taste
olive oil

Combine the mixed herbs with the egg yolks, 1¼ cups flour and ½ tablespoon salt in a food processor; process until mixed. Drizzle 1 teaspoon olive oil through the feed tube, processing constantly until the dough forms a ball. Wrap in plastic wrap and chill in the refrigerator for 1½ hours.

Knead the dough lightly on a floured surface, kneading in additional flour if the dough is sticky. Divide the dough into smaller portions and feed through a pasta maker, using the manufacturer's instructions, sprinkling the dough with flour each time it is run through the pasta maker. Let the pasta rest on a waxed paper-lined baking sheet in the refrigerator until ready to cook. Cook in boiling water with salt to taste and a splash of olive oil in a saucepan for 3 to 4 minutes. Drain and serve.

PASTRY CREAM

RATING: A Short Par 4; Low Greens Fees

MAKES: About 2 cups

Pastry cream is a standard base to which flavorings and other ingredients may be added to create many desserts. Left in its simplest state, pastry cream is also a tasty filling for sweet baked goods.

¾ cup sugar
¼ cup cornstarch
6 egg yolks
2 cups milk

Whisk the sugar, cornstarch and egg yolks together in a bowl. Bring the milk to a boil in a saucepan over medium-high heat. Whisk half the hot milk gradually into the egg yolk mixture to temper it. Return the remaining milk to the heat and return to a boil. Whisk in the egg mixture and return to a boil, whisking constantly and taking care to scrape the entire bottom of the saucepan. Pour the thickened mixture immediately into a bowl and place plastic wrap directly on the surface to prevent a skin from forming. Chill in the refrigerator.

Pâte au Choux
(Cream Puff Pastry Dough)

RATING: Par for the Course on a Par 4; Low Greens Fees

MAKES: 26 puffs

Sweet pastry dough is perfect for profiteroles or cream puffs, but with a few minor changes, it can be used in savory dishes. Just add a little grated cheese of your choice and reduce the amount of sugar by half for a classic gougère. Instead of filling the pastries with ice cream, whipped cream, or pastry cream, enjoy them on their own as elegant appetizers or fill the savory puffs with chicken salad, tuna salad, or a shellfish salad. This can also make a great hors d'oeuvre course or an elegant take on soup and finger sandwiches.

> 1 cup milk
> 1 cup water
> 2 tablespoons sugar
> 1 cup (2 sticks) butter
> 2 1/2 cups sifted flour
> 10 eggs

Preheat the oven to 425 degrees. Combine the milk, water, sugar and butter in a large saucepan and bring to a boil. Add the flour all at once and mix briskly with a wooden spoon. Cook for about 3 minutes or until the dough appears slightly dry and pulls easily from the side of the pan.

Transfer to a mixing bowl and mix at low speed with a paddle attachment for 10 minutes or until the mixture cools to room temperature.

Increase the mixer speed to medium and beat in the eggs 1 at a time, mixing well after each addition and scraping the side of the bowl frequently.

Spoon into a pastry bag and pipe the dough onto a parchment- or baking pad-lined baking sheet; you can also shape into 1- or 2-inch balls and place on the lined baking sheet.

Bake for 20 minutes or until puffed and beginning to brown; do no open the oven during the baking time, as a sudden change in oven temperature will deflate the puffs. Reduce the oven temperature to 375 degrees. Bake for 10 to 15 minutes longer or until the puffs appear dry. Remove to a wire rack to cool.

You can store uncooked dough in the refrigerator for up to 2 days. Shaped dough can be frozen on the baking sheets for 1 month. Do not thaw frozen dough before baking, but increase the cooking time slightly for frozen dough.

TIP: To create cream puff swans, pipe S shapes onto the baking sheet along with the round shapes. Slice the baked round puffs into halves horizontally. Spoon the filling into the bottom portions of the sliced puffs. Cut the top portions into halves and arrange on either side of the filled portions to resemble the wings. Stand the S in the filling for the swan's neck and head.

PÂTE BRISÉE
(BASIC PIE CRUST OR QUICHE CRUST)

RATING: A Long Par 4; Low Greens Fees

MAKES: 1 (9-inch) Tart Shell

This recipe calls for a hands-on approach. With all of the kitchen gadgetry available to us today, it is easy to forget about our most basic tools: our hands! Use your fingers to pinch the butter, use the heel of your hand to work the dough in the bowl, and again with your hands, shape the dough for resting.

2¹/4 cups flour
1 pinch of sugar
1 pinch of salt
3/4 cup (1¹/2 sticks) butter, chilled
¹/4 cup milk
1 egg, lightly beaten

Sift the flour, sugar and salt into a large bowl. Add the butter and pinch with your fingertips or use a pastry cutter to work the mixture into pea-size pieces. Add the milk and egg and mix just until a dough forms; some lumps of butter will remain.

Flatten the dough to a disk and wrap in plastic. Chill in the refrigerator for 2 hours or longer to allow the gluten in the flour to relax and form a tender dough.

Roll the dough ¹/8 inch thick on a floured cold surface. Transfer the dough to a 9-inch pie plate. Press into the plate and trim the edges. Rest the pastry in the refrigerator for 30 minutes.

Preheat the oven to 375 degrees. Prick the dough with a fork to allow steam to escape. Cover with a piece of foil cut to fit the pan, leaving a ¹/2-inch overhang. Fill with pie weights, dried beans or rice.

Bake the crust for 20 minutes or until the edges are golden brown and the center is set. Cool on a wire rack before filling.

PÂTE SUCRÉE (SUGAR DOUGH)

RATING: A Short Par 3; High Greens Fees

MAKES: 1 (11-inch) tart shell

It is easy to work with this dough, as it is not too sticky. Its distinctive component, hazelnut flour, should be made by finely grinding blanched hazelnuts.

2¹/4 cups all-purpose flour
¹/4 cup hazelnut flour
³/4 cup confectioners' sugar
2 eggs, lightly beaten
1¹/4 sticks butter, cut into ¹/2-inch cubes

Sift the all-purpose flour, hazelnut flour and confectioners' sugar into a mixing bowl. Add the eggs and mix at low speed. Add the butter gradually, increasing the mixer speed to medium and mixing until the mixture forms a ball.

Shape into a flattened disk and wrap in plastic wrap. Chill in the refrigerator for 2 hours to several days or store in the freezer for up to 1 month.

LEMON CURD

RATING: Par for the Course on a Par 3; Low Greens Fees

SERVES: 6

This makes for a decadent finish to a meal or pure satisfaction for an afternoon treat. Serve it in dessert cups with a dollop of whipped cream and a raspberry or as the filling for a lemon tart.

¹/2 cup fresh lemon juice
1¹/2 cups sugar
4 eggs
grated zest of ¹/2 of a lemon
1 cup (2 sticks) plus 1 tablespoon unsalted
    butter, chopped

Mix the lemon juice with ¹/2 of the sugar in a small bowl. Mix the remaining sugar with the eggs in a medium bowl. Add to the lemon juice mixture to the egg mixture and mix well. Stir in the lemon zest.

Spoon into a double boiler and cook over simmering water to 140 degrees on a candy thermometer. Add the butter gradually, mixing constantly until smooth. Spoon into a bowl and place plastic wrap directly on the surface. Cool to room temperature and chill in the refrigerator.

CRÈME BRÛLÉE

RATING: Par for the Course on a Par 4; High Greens Fees

SERVES: 10 to 12

A *food torch can be purchased for $24 to $40 at most hardware stores. Though a bit of an indulgence, it is the perfect tool to caramelize sugar, which is a needed to make the signature hard sugar shell that covers the rich custard cream within.*

1 quart (4 cups) heavy cream
1 cup milk
1 vanilla bean, split into halves lengthwise
2/3 cup sugar
9 egg yolks
2 whole eggs
10 to 12 tablespoons sugar

Preheat the oven to 350 degrees. Bring the cream, milk and vanilla bean to a boil over medium-high heat in a large saucepan.

Whisk 2/3 cup sugar, the egg yolks and whole eggs together in a large mixing bowl. Whisk in a portion of the heated cream mixture to temper the eggs and keep them from scrambling. Return the cream mixture to a boil.

Whisk the egg mixture into the heated cream and remove from the heat. Strain the mixture through a fine sieve and cool in an ice water bath.

Spoon into individual ramekins or shallow bowls. Place in a large baking pan and add enough boiling water to reach 2/3 of the way up the sides of the ramekins.

Bake for 20 minutes or until the custards just tremble when the larger pan is shaken. Cool the custards and wrap in plastic wrap. Store in the refrigerator.

Sprinkle each ramekin with 1 tablespoon of the sugar, covering the entire surface. Caramelize the sugar with a food torch and serve immediately.

TIP: Look for a plump vanilla bean, one that has not dried out. This will ensure the maximum flavor and make it much easier to split the bean lengthwise. When using the food torch to caramelize the sugar, work the flame uniformly across the surface of the sugar. As soon as bubbles appear, move the flame to the next area, or the sugar will burn.

INDEX

INDEX

INDEX

To order additional copies of
The Fairway Gourmet
or for more information, please visit
www.thefairwaygourmet.com or www.plutonrestaurant.com,
or write to
The Fairway Gourmet
1235 A North Clybourn #351
Chicago, Illinois 60610